Danger
Ahead

Danger Ahead

The Risks You *Really* Face on Life's Highway

LARRY LAUDAN

John Wiley & Sons, Inc.

New York • Chichester • Weinheim • Brisbane • Singapore • Toronto

Library of Congress Cataloging-in-Publication Data
Laudan, Larry
    Danger ahead : the risks you *really* face on life's highway / Larry
Laudan.
    p. cm.
    Includes index.
    ISBN 0-471-13440-6 (pbk. : alk. paper)
    1. Risk perception—United States—Statistics. 2. Risk
assessment—United States—Statistics. I. Title.
HM256.L382 1997
302'.12—dc21   97-9920

Printed in the United States of America
10 9 8 7 6 5 4 3 2 1

To Marilyn and Ken,
fellow risk-runners.

Contents

Danger
Ahead

1

Laws for Avoiding Risk-Lock

A decade ago, I knew no more about risks than the next person. Although my duties as a philosopher of science saw me teaching courses in esoteric topics like probability and statistics from time to time, my interest in risks was largely theoretical. The dawning of my practical interest in risky subjects can be dated with some precision. It was a morning in May 1989. As usual, I opened the morning newspaper over breakfast; there on the front page was a headline screaming that a new study had shown that coffee might cause bladder cancer.

Up until then, like most of us, I had been trying to keep a running mental tally of what was safe and what was not. I knew that fat was bad for you; so was alcohol, except maybe red wine. Smoked meats were to be avoided. Fish, especially shellfish, might be contaminated, but fatty fish was healthy. Oat bran and nuts were a plus. Smoking was not. Seat belts and air bags—the latter just then appearing on the scene— were good, but small cars were risky. Aspirin irritated the stomach but possibly prevented strokes. Exercise was good for you, provided it didn't kill you. Junk bonds were dicey but carried impressive returns. Government bonds were solid but barely beat inflation. Sex was healthy, but only with a condom.

Having a lot of sex lowered the risk of ovarian cancer but increased the chances of cervical cancer. Air travel was, everybody said, safe—unless one were traveling in a private plane, in which case it was very dangerous. Green, naturally grown vegetables were good, red meat was bad, and so on and so forth.

As I tried to force my brain to add coffee to its already vast list of suspect substances, it suddenly rebelled. I began suffering from what I have come to call *risk-lock*. Like gridlock, this condition renders us incapable of doing anything or going anywhere. If—as I then thought—more or less everything is risky, then risk avoidance is not a viable strategy. If risks are unavoidable, then what does it matter what I do or don't do? I decided then and there that the thing to do was to prioritize the risks. Avoid the stuff that was most dangerous and not worry about the mild risks.

It then dawned on me that although I carried around in my head this impressive inventory of possibly risky things and activities, I hadn't a clue which risks were greater than others. I began to realize that magazines and newspapers and television, which had been feeding me this steady stream of stories about risky things, had utterly failed to provide any idea about what was seriously dangerous and what was only trivially risky. If some activity were going to expose me to a 1 in 100 or 1 in 1,000 chance of coming to a nasty end, then I'd try to avoid it; if the risk was closer to, say, 1 in 10 million, I wasn't going to worry about it.

The problem, as I said, was that the media were not telling me what I needed to know to sort out the serious risks from the barely niggling ones. It was then that I embarked on a project of trying to learn what the real levels of risks are.

For almost a decade, I have been doing precisely that. This book is one fruit of those efforts. I wrote it because I suppose that many others find themselves in the same tragicomic conundrum as I did. They know enough to realize that many things are risky but not enough to know which risks are the central and serious ones. Its aim is not to frighten. Far from it, it is meant as a guide for how to avoid paranoia in a world where everyone is telling you that almost everything you do involves putting your life on the line. Later chapters will present much of the relevant information about the risks of ordinary life. In this chapter, I want to mention some general principles that I have gleaned from wading through the professional literature on risk. Immodestly, I call these nineteen principles Laudan's Laws.

FIRST LAW: EVERYTHING IS RISKY

The first of these principles is the easiest to state but probably the hardest to adjust to. The media are, for once, right: nothing—absolutely nothing—is completely safe. Risks lurk everywhere. Driving to work in the morning may put you in the traffic fatalities column. Staying home in bed may make you one of the half million Americans each year who require emergency room treatment for an injury sustained by falling out of bed. There is no food, no activity, no *in*activity—however innocuous it may seem—that is without its potential to inflict harm. Fifty children a year drown in the familiar 5-gallon buckets that adorn almost every basement or washroom. Ten people a year accidentally hang themselves on the cords of their draperies or venetian blinds. Tens of thousands of us each year go to emergency rooms for treatment of wounds caused by handling money—everything here from deep paper cuts to (for the very rich) hernias. Businesses and individuals go bankrupt at an alarming rate.

I begin with this premise of the ubiquity of risk not so as to wallow in the paranoia that voicing it sometimes provokes. Rather, I want to be able to move beyond it—for a sensible attitude to the risks of everyday life depends on getting a perspective. One key part of that perspective involves the realization that, because nothing is "safe" (if safe means risk-free), we have to pick our way through life seeking to minimize risks rather than to eliminate them. Such minimizing requires us to know how various things stack up against one another in terms of their *relative* risk.

SECOND LAW:
REJECT THE MYTH THAT WE
LIVE IN ESPECIALLY RISKY TIMES

A recent study of the content of U.S. daily newspapers showed that fully 35% of all stories—and about 47% of front-page stories—deal with the risks of modern life. If it's not crime, it's pollution. If it's not our diet, it's an economic catastrophe. We've been warned about radon, chlorinated water, pesticide residues, vaccinations, cholesterol in the diet, the impending stock market collapse, killer plagues like *Ebola*, and earthquakes and hurricanes, to name but a few.

Under the circumstances, it's easy to suppose that life is much more hazardous now than it used to be. After all, half a century ago, no one fretted about carcinogens, asbestos, the ozone layer, pesticides, lead paint, and many other recently discovered dangers. But although no one worried about these dangers—after all, they didn't even know what the danger was—the fact is that life now is a great deal less risky than it ever was, even a generation ago. The numbers make this vividly clear. If life in the United States were riskier now than

---

FACTORS OF 10

As the figures in this book show, risks vary enormously from one case to another. One way to define a level of tolerance for yourself is by considering how far down this list you would have to go before you felt that a risk was trivial. Each level here represents a decrease by a power of 10:

Lifetime Risks

Killed by Heart Attack (risk: 1 in 3)

Killed in Car Accident (1 in 42)

Killed by Fall (1 in 380)

Killed in Plane Crash (1 in 4,000)

Killed by Lightning (1 in 35,000)

Killed by a Plane Falling on You (1 in 300,000)

Killed by Rabies (1 in 2 million)

---

it used to be, mortality and accident rates should be increasing and life expectancies should be dropping (as they are in Russia). Quite the opposite is true.

Americans are living longer than ever—almost a decade longer than folks at the turn of the century. The rate of death due to accidents, whether at home or on the job, is barely one-third what it was in the 1930s. Mile for mile, driving is twice as safe as it was only a generation ago. If a few new serious risks have emerged (the most obvious is AIDS), many others have waned. Virtually gone are smallpox, polio, diphtheria, and malaria—classic killers of the last 100 years. As for that other apparently modern risk, pollution, the truth is that the air and the water in the United States are cleaner now than they were when agencies first began monitoring their quality earlier this century.

If, as I claim, everything is getting better on the risk front, why do risks and dangers loom so much larger in public discussion than they used to? The key answer is that we can now detect many very low level statistical risks that eluded previous techniques of investigation. Especially important here has been the development of the techniques of epidemiology. This discipline can detect harms that operate along invisible pathways or that, like cancer, take decades to develop. Fully half the risks we now recognize were identified using this new tool. Most of these minuscule risks were there all along, of course, but were invisible to the techniques of analysis and detection available earlier.

So, everything is risky but almost everything is safer than it used to be. If you're a pessimist, you tend to fixate on the former; if an optimist, the latter. But both are true and both should play a key role in figuring out your own attitudes toward risk and safety. Unfortunately, adopting a sensible attitude toward lifestyle choices by informing yourself about the levels of risks is made more difficult because of the Third Law.

THIRD LAW:
MANY OPINION SHAPERS EXAGGERATE RISKS

There are now large groups of people who have a vested interest in keeping us on our guard about risks—often to the point of exaggerating them out of all proportion. We all know this about certain industries that have a stake in selling us something to reduce our risk—whether it is an insurance policy or a smoke detector. But industry is not the only, probably not even the major, player in this game.

The media, for instance, want to sell newspapers or gain viewers. Stories about how dangerous life is pique viewer or reader interest every bit as much as a juicy scandal. A scientist has barely to breathe a word about a new study of, say, diet risks, and it becomes front-page news in every city— especially if it finds a link, however remote, between cancer or heart disease and some factor we had not expected, like drinking coffee or living near power lines or using a cellular phone.

But industry spokesmen and journalists are by no means the only ones with an incentive for hawking risks. Sizable chunks of the government bureaucracy (for example, in the Centers for Disease Control, the Occupational Health and Safety Administration, the National Institutes of Health, the Consumer Product Safety Commission, and the Environmental Protection Agency) have jobs whose continued funding depends on the existence of a public perception that we face grave risks that these agencies must monitor and regulate.

The Centers for Disease Control is an interesting case in point. Originally set up specifically to monitor infectious diseases, its enviable success at that enterprise has created a problem of function. Because smallpox, diphtheria, rabies, polio, and many other infectious diseases are rapidly vanishing, agencies like the CDC can preserve their size and their importance only by identifying new missions—in effect reinventing themselves. And a central part of that redefinition involves directing the searchlight of public attention to many risks that are either obscure or well outside the original mandate of the organization. In fact, at the CDC, only one of its current seven divisions is concerned with the original mission of the organization. The public servants who work in the risk field, usually with extensive scientific training, have too much integrity to invent risks out of whole cloth. But they can hardly be expected to soft-pedal what risks they do find, especially when—as is commonly true with very low level risks—there is plenty of room for divergent interpretation of the data.

Outside the government itself, there are entire industries with a financial stake in risk management of various sorts. Environmentalists, especially the professional sort, likewise have a strong vested interest in persuading the rest of us that the world is going to come to a nasty end unless we support their efforts with a fat donation. Lawyers, ever keen on the fat commission, are motivated to find or invent all manner of risks (for example, they led the brouhahas over silicone breast implants and Agent Orange), even where relevant scientific evidence to support the risk claims is lacking. The moral here is clear: Whenever some group or organization begins alarming talk about some new risk, ask yourself what it has to gain before you take its claims at face value.

FOURTH LAW: ALWAYS MAKE COMPARISONS

Is flying dangerous? If that question means "Might I die if I fly?" then the answer is obvious. But the relevant question, of course, is a different one: Do I risk more taking a plane than by driving or taking a train? In general, flying is safer, although (as we shall see later on) the story is more complicated than that. It depends, among other things, on how far you are flying, what kind of driver you are, what sort of airline you use, and what vehicle you drive. The point is that it makes no sense to discuss the safety of air travel in a vacuum, separated from a consideration of the alternatives.

Is it dangerous to eat broiled steaks? Well, yes—in the sense that anything *could* harm you. But is it dangerous enough to cause us to worry about getting cancer from eating broiled steaks once or twice a week for a lifetime? Think of it this way: You are more likely to be die by choking to death on a steak than by consuming the carcinogens it acquired during the heating process. If you don't spend sleepless nights worrying about fatally choking on your food, then you probably shouldn't give a second thought to whether your T-bone is charbroiled. The issue here is not whether smoked meats are dangerous but, rather, how that danger stacks up against others.

Most of us have heard that peanut butter contains a carcinogen called aflatoxin. Fearful of cancer, some have shied away from peanut butter in recent years. What they do not take into their calculations is that carcinogens are everywhere in our diet. Ethyl alcohol (as in beer, wine, and whiskey) is a known human carcinogen. Almost all fruits contain chemicals that produce tumors in rodents. So, too, does broccoli, coffee, and half of the other foods we consume without giving them an extra thought. I am *not* referring here to the carcinogens carried by the pesticide residues on foods. This is the naturally occurring stuff. If you seriously sought to avoid everything that contained suspected or known human carcinogens, your diet would not only be drastically restricted but it would also be enormously *unhealthy*—because many carcinogen-carrying fruits and vegetables contain important nutrients, some of which are hard to obtain in other ways.

This book aims to give you the data to begin making informed, comparative choices in your life. It will emphatically drive home the point that the right question is *never* "Is this safe?" but, rather, "How risky is it?"

FIFTH LAW: MANY HIGH-PROFILE RISKS DON'T MATTER MUCH

As this book will illustrate over and over again, most of the things that the media have encouraged us to be afraid of

are about as safe as anything can be. Consider our stereotype
of risky jobs. High on most people's list would be the police
officer. We have all watched video images of those somber
funerals for fallen cops and pondered the courage it must take
to walk the beat day after day. Well, in reality, being a police
officer is much less risky than many other ordinary jobs. For
instance, you are more likely to die on the job as a farmer or
a truck driver than as a cop. Adding insult to injury, the
evidence shows that about half of slain police officers are
accidentally shot by other officers rather than by the crooks.

Then there is that recently touted villain, secondary
tobacco smoke. Does it kill? Yes. Does it produce respiratory
disease in some children? Again, yes. For such reasons, many
smoking parents have been exiled to the chilly front porch so
as to avoid creating respiratory problems for their children.
Health officials, unwilling to set *any* risk in context, do not
bother to point out to parents that the level of respiratory risk
posed to little Johnny by Mommy's smoking is less than little
Johnny will suffer if Mommy has another baby. The number
and severity of respiratory illnesses suffered by the children in
a nonsmoking family of five (rather than three) are greater
than that suffered by a single child in a smoking household of
three. It is easy to understand why: more children in the
household mean drastically more childhood disease germs in
circulation.

Typically, these same parents will also go to great pains to
make their homes more energy-efficient, having been urged
on by the media to minimize our dependency on foreign oil.
They may be blissfully ignorant of the degree to which a well-
sealed home acts as a sink for bacteria, viruses, and allergens.
Since (or so I suppose) no family hesitates for a second about
having a second child because that will marginally expose the
existing child(ren) to the greater risk of disease, and no

family decides against weatherstripping their doors even though there is a risk that it will increase disease, they might want to rethink the isolation ward mentality about smoking in the household. Here again, the important thing is not whether there is a risk, but how big it is and how it compares with other things we do or might do.

SIXTH LAW:
AVOID THE BIG RISKS AND THE SMALL ONES WILL TAKE CARE OF THEMSELVES

As John Maynard Keynes wisely quipped, in the long run, we are all dead. The principal risk question for most of us is how long we can postpone the inevitable. To answer that, we need to remind ourselves that the principal killers of North Americans are heart attacks, cancer, and strokes. One obvious way of making it likely you will live longer is by doing what you can to protect yourself from these three killers. Although, as we will see later, the story is complicated in its details, the general picture is clear enough. What you eat, whether you smoke, how much if any alcohol you drink are the three biggest factors within your control of your susceptibility to these fatal diseases. Exercise is also a factor, although it does not rank among the top three. So are heredity, lifestyle, and your standard of living.

> **RISK GEOGRAPHY**
>
> U.S. city in which you are most likely to be living alone: Washington, D.C.

The big three diseases are generally the afflictions of late middle age and old age, but there are several killers that strike people at much earlier ages. These include AIDS, homicide, suicide, and accidents—especially motor vehicle accidents.

Among them, these claim some 200,000 lives every year, deaths that are especially tragic because they snuff out persons of every age, including the very young. Figures discussed later in this book will help you identify who is most at risk to fall prey to these threats.

Let's suppose that you inform yourself about some of the hundreds of risks described in later pages. Is that enough? Knowing what the risks are, and how large they are, turns out to be just the first step. Beyond the bare risks themselves, most of us want to know how to avoid them or, at a minimum, how to reduce them. This is especially important, as the Seventh Law demonstrates.

SEVENTH LAW:
THE OBVIOUS SOLUTIONS
ARE OFTEN THE WRONG ONES

If we're concerned about deaths on the highways, we might try lowering the speed limit or mandating air bags for new vehicles. The troubles with lowering the speed limit on highways is a good case in point. It only stands to reason that if you lower the speed limits people will have fewer crashes and those that do occur will be less severe. Sounds good, right? Well, difficulties abound. One is economic. If people and goods move along roads at significantly lower speeds, the wheels of commerce and ordinary life turn more slowly. Trucking companies require more time to deliver shipments. Delivery drivers can cover less of their route than previously. There are obvious costs associated with lowering speed limits.

Surely, you say, we should be prepared to pay whatever it costs if this means saving lives. The logic of that argument quickly peters out. Because if it is true, say, that reducing speeds from 65 to 55 miles per hour saves lives, and it is, then it equally stands to reason that reducing them further to 45 or 35 or 25 miles per hour would save even more lives. At some point, even the most compassionate critic of deaths on the highways will concede that the costs in terms of the economy and personal inconvenience more than outweigh the gains in lives saved. The tricky question is where to draw that line.

But things turn out to be even more complicated. So far, we have supposed that if we lower the speed limits people will drive more slowly. There is little evidence that this is so. It is everyone's experience, borne out by dozens of scientific studies, that only a minority of cars on the highways drives at or below the posted speed limits. And the lower the posted speed limits, the larger the proportion of persons who ignore them. On U.S. highways today, for instance, most motorists are technically speeding most of the time. It seems that most drivers have an intuitive sense of what is a safe speed for given road and weather conditions and drive at that speed, regardless of the posted speed limits. Apart from the fact that posted limits do not impact driving speeds as dramatically as the authorities would like, we have to reckon with another cost here: namely, the indifference to, bordering on contempt for, the law that is created when laws are passed that make most citizens lawbreakers.

Maybe we could tackle the problem another way. If we can't make drivers slow down, perhaps we could make their vehicles more likely to avoid a fatal crash. Let's install air bags and seat belts, fit them with antilock brake systems, and encourage drivers to buy larger cars (which always survive better than small cars in crashworthy tests). All of these measures have produced discouraging results, and the reason is not difficult to see. Plenty of evidence indicates that if you put someone in a heavy car who is accustomed to driving a light one, he drives faster. If you give someone antilock brakes and put her on slippery roads, she will drive faster than her counterpart without the fancy brakes. Drivers with air bags drive, on average, a bit faster than those without.

In each of these cases, what appears to be going on is that the driver is making a rational calculation. He is saying to himself, "I'm safer in a bigger car, with air bags, with antilock brakes, so I can drive just a bit faster because I've taken all these precautions." The effect is that many of the risk-avoidance advantages of these safety features are frittered away because they encourage a greater indifference to risk. The point is that what appear on paper to be good solutions to problems of risk often turn out not to be because their effect is canceled out by the risk-taker's implicit calculation of his new situation.

EIGHTH LAW:
ALWAYS FIND OUT THE BASE RATE

Suppose you saw this headline in your local paper:

RABIES DEATHS TO DOUBLE IN DECADE:
Mexican Squirrel Crosses the Rio Grande

The accompanying story explains that a scientist has discovered that a certain Central American mammal is slowly working its way north, poised to cross the Rio Grande. She has good epidemiological evidence that when this squirrel establishes itself in the United States, the number of children who die of rabies will *double* by 2005.

Such news would make banner headlines across the country. Congress would appropriate millions to prevent this unwelcome invasion. Parents, especially in southwestern states, would be demanding that local health authorities do something to control the menace. Local television anchors would interview anxious mothers about the problem. Public television would follow up with a 1-hour special on the cruelty of the countermeasures taken to control the squirrel population.

There is no such creature, but the point is that even if there were, the panic would be completely misplaced. Strange as it may seem, in a *bad* year one or two Americans nationwide die from rabies. (In 1991, no one died of rabies.) This average is *the base rate*, and risks are meaningless if you don't know the base rate. Doubling the base rate here would increase the number of rabies deaths to between two and four—still virtually negligible. Even at these heightened levels of risk, Americans would be much more likely to die of an airplane falling on them than from rabies. Once we know what the rabies base rate is, we can see that a doubling or trebling would still pose little or no threat to public mortality. But if all we know is that something threatens to double a risk or worse, we tend—egged on by newspaper headlines—to suppose that we are facing a serious public health crisis that requires both vigilant attention and decisive action.

Unfortunately, much press coverage of health and consumer risks focuses on the risk multiplier without telling us anything about the base rate. Within the last couple of years, for instance, headlines have screamed that the use of certain garden pesticides may increase the risk of childhood leukemia two- or threefold. The Environmental Protection Agency has told us that exposure to secondary smoke increases a nonsmoker's risk of fatal lung cancer by perhaps 30%. This sounds awful.

What few bothered to point out was that childhood leukemia is a very rare disease to begin with (about 1 child in 80,000 dies of leukemia in a given year) and that the incidence of lung cancer among nonsmokers with no exposure to secondary smoke is very low (roughly 1 death per 100,000+

adults per year). Even if it is true that pesticides increase leukemia rates and that secondary smoke marginally increases lung cancer rates among nonsmokers, this may not be cause for major alarm, *if* the base rates are sufficiently low. Doubling a risk of 1 in 10 is terrifying; doubling a risk of 1 in 1 million is not.

The same pattern of half-truths driving decision making occurred during the hoopla about cancer risk to children in classrooms with asbestos insulation. Researchers noted that exposure to asbestos fibers "significantly" increased the risk of developing mesothelioma later in life. In response to these much-publicized studies, and urged on by the Environmental Protection Agency, local school districts have spent billions on asbestos-removal projects. Few influential voices bothered pointing out that, at worst, the lifetime risk of dying from this disease because of classroom asbestos exposure is about the same as the lifetime risk of dying from cancer caused by drinking tap water in the average U.S. home—where the annual risk is less than 1 in 1 million.

Of course, to the individual dying from rabies or leukemia, it is small comfort to know that one's affliction is a statistical fluke. But for the rest of us, these risks pale by comparison with ones that are far more likely to do us in. We can make sensible decisions about what risks to tackle only if we can distinguish the serious risks from the remote or trivial ones. Without a knowledge of base rates, such decisions are impossible.

It is sheer folly to try to avoid everything that might harm us, because virtually everything might. What we need, as decision makers and consumers, is information about how one risk stacks up against others. The media resolutely resist providing such truth in advertising, probably because it would undermine their ability to generate front-page headlines or lead features from the discovery of new, and often marginal, risks. But a good general rule of thumb is this: If the scare-mongers don't give you a base rate for their favorite risk-of-the-month, you probably needn't rush to change your lifestyle. As in baseball, so in risk management: Where there's no baseline, everything is a foul.

NINTH LAW:
DON'T TAKE AUNT MOLLY'S WORD FOR IT

You buy a replacement battery for your car. While installing it, you notice, too late, that it is leaking corrosive acid, which is now smeared over both hands. Six months later you take the manufacturer to court. At trial, you tell your tale of the leaking battery and you display your scarred palms. You saw how the accident happened and you have the scars to prove it. An open-and-shut case. You'll win a handsome award and are fully entitled to it.

Suppose instead that you are a highway trooper, suffering from testicular cancer. You file suit against the manufacturer of your radar gun, claiming that years of laying the gun across your lap caused your condition. Or suppose you live close to high-voltage transmission lines, subsequently develop a brain tumor, and take the electric company to court. Or you live 50 miles downwind of a nuclear power plant and note that two families in your neighborhood, including your own, develop mysterious symptoms; you sue the company that built the reactor.

None of these other cases is like the battery acid one, despite apparent parallels, for in them, although certainly worse off than you were before, you are in no position to determine what caused your malady. The pathways of causation here are invisible. The highway patrolman may be utterly convinced that the radar gun did it, but, although he knows he used such a gun and that he now has cancer, his guess about the link between the two is utterly worthless. In each of these situations, we are dealing with what is called *anecdotal* evidence.

The only way to find out whether radar guns or high voltages really are causing cancer is to use the sophisticated tools of epidemiology and statistical analysis. These require the scrutiny of hundreds of cases and the careful design of trials that will screen out other possible causes. Until and unless such techniques are brought to bear, anecdotal evidence should carry no force.

But carry force it does, especially with the media, which delight in turning anecdotal allegations of blame into proven indictments. Examples abound in practically every television newscast, but the best known instance of anecdotal evidence fueling a national frenzy about risks was the infamous Love Canal case.

It began in 1976 when residents near Love Canal in Niagara, New York, started reporting a series of horrible maladies. The canal itself had been used in the 1940s and 1950s as a dump site for hazardous chemical wastes by Hooker Chemical Company. By the late 1970s, Love Canal had become a media circus, with weekly visits from network correspondents, interviewing hysterical residents about the catalog of diseases they were suffering. It was impressive indeed: numerous cancers in the neighborhood, birth defects, spontaneously aborted pregnancies, epilepsy, and so forth. And each resident "knew" that the chemical wastes in the canal caused their problems. Because of the national hue and cry, almost 500 families were moved out permanently in 1978.

After all the hoopla, those with the tools to get to the bottom of it were finally brought in. The conclusion they reached was that the incidence of serious disease in the vicinity of Love Canal was not significantly greater than in any other U.S. suburb. As the *New York Times* summarized the findings of the scientists in 1981: "From what is now known, Love Canal, perhaps the nation's most prominent symbol of chemical assaults on the environment, has had no detectable effect on the incidence of cancer." It was, by the way, Love Canal and a handful of similar occurrences that gave us the federal Superfund legislation (which costs about $15 billion per year).

How can individuals be so wrong about what ails them? The cruel fact is that having cancer does not give one a special knowledge of how one acquired it. A second factor is that diseases like cancer are very common. Since roughly 1 in 3 Americans will develop cancer at some time in their lives, it is scarcely surprising if any neighborhood, such as Love Canal, develops several cases in quick succession. The power of suggestion is potent in these circumstances.

We should resist the idea that individual testimony can prove anything in such cases. It cannot. However heartrending and telegenic, anecdotal evidence is putting 2 and 2 together to get 5.

TENTH LAW:
RISKS THAT SCIENTISTS CALL
"SIGNIFICANT" USUALLY AREN'T

Practically every day brings new headlines to the effect that scientists have discovered yet another significant link between some activity (eating smoked meat, for example) and some harm (such as cancer). The unwary, on learning that the link is "significant," naturally enough assume that it must be important. After all, that is what the term means in plain English.

But when scientists use such language, they have a very different idea in mind. When a scientist says that a link or causal connection is "significant," she simply means that she is 95% sure (more or less) that the two sorts of events are *somehow* connected. What she does *not* necessarily mean—although it is easy enough to misread it this way—is that you will probably suffer harm if you engage in the activity in question.

Suppose, for instance, that someone is investigating a possible link between drinking milk and cancer of the pancreas. He discovers that milk drinkers are 0.1% more likely to develop pancreatic cancer than someone who never touches the stuff. Now, this result may well be "significant" in the scientist's sense. Provided that the size of the sample is large enough, even such tiny effects can satisfy the statistician's sense of significance.

To all the rest of us, however, this result is absolutely trivial and of no importance. Because pancreatic cancer itself is rare, a small elevation in its probability due to milk-drinking will mean it is still a rare event, even among lifelong milk drinkers. Knowing that a lifetime of milk-drinking increases the chances of your developing cancer by one-tenth of 1% will not, and should not, frighten you into changing your habits. On the other hand, if all you are told is simply that there is a significant link between milk and cancer, you are likely to suppose that this is a big-time connection, requiring some sort of action of your part.

The antidote to such panic is the realization that significance in the statistical sense is *never* an indication of the size or magnitude of a risk; it is, rather, an indication of the confidence of the scientist that there is some link or other, even if that link is vanishingly small.

Why then should it matter whether the results of a study

are "significant"? Well, it is not irrelevant information because it can alert scientists to what may be theoretically interesting issues. But because significant linkages can also be negligible ones (in terms of their size), it is never enough to know that scientists have found significant results.

When a scientist wants to say that something is significant (in the plain English sense of that term), she will tell you that there is an uncomfortably high probability that if you engage in such-and-such activity then you will be harmed. But most risk studies that find their ways into the pages of newspapers are not of that sort. Whether out of ignorance or a predilection for selling papers, journalists are apt to act as if a significant risk always represents a grave danger. This is to confuse apples and oranges. No, it's much worse than that, because here the confusion can be between the harmful and the virtually harmless.

The moral is plain: Find out what the level of a risk is before you start worrying about it. Merely knowing that it is "statistically significant" should *never* be a cause for alarm.

> **RISK GEOGRAPHY**
>
> In 1986, Lake Nyos in Cameroon released a cloud of carbon monoxide. More than 1,700 people living nearby were killed instantly.

A related point is worth making in passing. Even when scientists have established a "significant" link, there is still plenty of room for error and doubt. In fact, we know for sure that if scientists are working with a so-called 5% margin of error, which is customary in risk research, then 1 in every 20 studies that "proves" a significant risk is a false-positive; that is, *it has found a link that does not exist.* When scientists use wider error margins, such as 10% (as they did, for instance, in the Environmental Protection Agency's landmark study on passive smoking), they increase to 1 in 10 the chances that a particular study reporting a significant link has found, in fact, nothing but an artifact of the statistics.

ELEVENTH LAW:
THE FAILURE TO FIND A RISK
DOESN'T MEAN THAT THERE ISN'T ONE

I often find myself in the happy position of being able to tell friends that the world is a good deal safer than some of them have supposed. The message here is rather the reverse: certain things may be a good deal riskier than you have imagined.

Earlier, I pointed out that it was easy to mistake the claim that some risk was "significant" with the idea that it was major or important. Scientists often find statistically significant risks that are nonetheless negligible. My advice then was, Don't worry about a risk merely because it is significant.

Well, there is a flip side to the story. Sometimes, after studying a drug or chemical or activity, scientists will announce that they have found no significant risk associated with it. Does that mean it's safe? Unfortunately, no.

So, there is reason to be wary when a spokesman for a company marketing potentially risky products insists that "studies show that there is no significant risk from using this product." Usually, the studies in question show nothing of the sort. Typically, the studies in question simply failed to find a significant risk associated with using the product. Here, the failure to find such a risk is not necessarily good evidence that there is none.

If this is a little confusing, think of how verdicts work in criminal law. There, the burden is on the prosecution to prove the defendant's guilt beyond a reasonable doubt. Even if a juror suspects that a defendant is guilty, the juror must still find the defendant innocent unless the case for guilt is over-whelming.

The risk analyst faces a similar problem. Before she can pronounce some product or activity a "significant" risk, she must be very sure (usually 95% sure) that there is a real connection between the risk and some well-defined harm. Even if her data lead her to suspect a linkage, she must report that no risk has been found unless the case for the linkage is statistically very powerful. For that reason, the verdict "not known to be risky" no more means "probably safe" than "not guilty" means "probably innocent."

Even when an investigator has no specific reasons for sus-pecting risk, it may be there nonetheless. For instance, a phar-maceutical company may conduct very thorough studies on a new drug, using a sample of, say, 5,000 volunteers. No nasty side effects are detected, so the company begins mass pro-duction and sale of the drug, which appears safe. Years later, the manufacturer may well discover that 1 in every 20,000 users has a fatal reaction to the drug. Such rare events would almost certainly elude the preliminary testing, however well designed the clinical trial was.

Epidemiological studies are generally even less sensitive than clinical trials. Typically, a risk will not show up as genuine in an epidemiological study unless the product under study produces an increased risk of 100% or more above the base rate. This means that if some new hair dryer increases the risk of electrical shock by 20%, epidemiological research almost certainly could not detect it. The researcher would have to report "no significant risk," even though the risk was genuine.

As our tools of analysis become more sensitive, we are able to detect risks that eluded the investigators of a genera-tion ago. That is one reason why the world seems much more risky now than it used to. Risks have not increased; generally, quite the opposite. But our enhanced ability to detect risks forces us to see that many things that once seemed fully safe are not so. Those abilities are still acutely limited, however. That is why—despite all the precautions built into the testing of drugs and many other consumer products—the old adage still applies: Let the buyer beware!

TWELFTH LAW:
SAFETY STANDARDS ARE INCONSISTENT

Everyone agrees that the government has a right to step in to protect us from risks imposed by others. The watchdog work of the Food and Drug Administration and the Consumer Products Safety Commission is a perfect example. Most of us might even agree that government has the right to legislate so as to protect us from the risks we impose on ourselves; that's the point of seat belt laws for motorists or mandatory helmet requirements for cyclists. Because we do generally expect Washington or the states to protect us from risk, it is no surprise that one-third of all government regulations are risk management—related in one way or another.

> **RISK GEOGRAPHY**
>
> State where a teenager is most likely to meet a violent end: Washington, D.C. (1 in 500 teenagers each year). Least likely: New Jersey (1 in 2,000 each year).

There is a third thing that most of us would agree about: that the government should be evenhanded in its definition of the risks that require legislative or administrative regulation. Permitting highly risky activities, while forbidding less risky ones, would seem to be a crazy and egregious abuse of government authority. Yet it is impossible to look at the maze of governmental risk control activities without concluding that something of this sort has gone badly astray.

Consider a few examples. Suppose that you're tooling down the highway in the family minivan. No passengers, just yourself. The van is fitted with air bags (as all new passenger cars after 1997 will have to be). You debate about whether to fasten your seat belt and decide to ride on the wild side; after all, that's why you laid out $800 for the air bags. As you drive along, the guy passing you right now happens to be on a motorcycle. He's followed by a beat-up pickup, with three farm workers riding in the back.

Two minutes later, a state trooper pulls you over and gives you a citation for not wearing a seat belt. You point out to him that riding a motorbike or in the back of a pickup is much (and I mean *much*) more dangerous than riding in a car without a seat belt. The trooper has seen enough nasty crashes to agree with you but reminds you that what they did was legal whereas you were breaking the law. End of discussion.

Clearly, something is out of whack here. If a state permits people to ride motorcycles (all do, many not even requiring a helmet) and permits passengers in the bed of a pickup (and many do), then what possible grounds can the state have for making car drivers, especially in cars with air bags, buckle up? Well, as the public service ads tell us, "It saves lives." Indeed it does, but then so would prohibiting all traffic above 5 miles per hour. If we do not ban motorbikes and pickups, we ought not be banning the car driver who does not use a belt.

The feds require seat belts on airplanes but not on passenger trains or buses. They demand infant seats in cars but not on planes. What's troubling here is that the state is bringing totally different standards to bear in deciding which risks to condone and which to proscribe. In this particular case, the inconsistencies create little more than a minor nuisance and mild irritation to car drivers who know that, legal or not, buckled up or not, they're a great deal safer than other travelers are.

But in other areas of our lives, such inconsistent handling of risk policy creates some anomalies and injustices. By federal law, for instance, a farmer cannot use more than a certain level of pesticides on crops because of the risk of carcinogenic residues in the food that finds its way to consumers. Ponder, now, his organic farming neighbor. Opposed to the use of pesticides, the latter chooses to grow crop or plant varieties that have much higher natural carcinogenic levels. (They pretty well have to have this added protection because the organic farmer needs to use strains with high natural levels of pest-resistance.) The government tells the first farmer that he cannot sell his produce at the market unless the detectable residues are less than a few parts per million, but the organic farmer can, without the slightest hint of governmental intervention, market his produce—even if it is in fact much more carcinogenic to those who consume it.

The same thing happens farther along the food chain. A firm that sells peanut butter cannot color it brown using a certain dye because that dye has been found to be ever so mildly carcinogenic. The fact that the natural carcinogens in peanut butter are several thousand times more numerous than the carcinogens in the dye doesn't figure in federal calculations. Similarly, a cake manufacturer is prohibited from adding a certain chemical preservative to her products in order to prolong their shelf life. The reason? The preservative is a *suspected* carcinogen. Yet the same cake maker can add brandy to preserve her spice cake, without provoking the batting of a federal eyelash, even though alcohol is a *known* human carcinogen. Here, we prohibit a possible carcinogen and permit a known one simply because alcohol has been around long enough that none of us thinks of it as a chemical additive.

THIRTEENTH LAW:
REDUCING RISKS DOES NOT BENEFIT EVERYONE

A zero-sum game is one in which there are both winners and losers. It's often said that risk reduction is not like that—that *everyone* profits when we reduce risks of illness, injury, and death. Indeed, one reason why there is such a strong consensus behind the government playing a role in curtailing risks is precisely because we suppose that everyone benefits. Unfortunately, risk reduction efforts are not always so equitable. Sometimes, reducing one person's risks brings new and unwelcome risks to others.

Consider a typical case. For several decades, there has been strong evidence that passengers in large cars are more likely to survive a highway crash than those in small cars. Many safety authorities—mindful of these facts—have urged buyers to invest in the largest car they can afford. Good for everybody, right?

Actually, no. The pedestrian, for one, stands to lose a great deal. The severity of an injury to a pedestrian, as well as the probability than he or she will be fatally injured when hit by a car, largely depends on the momentum of the moving vehicle. Because an object's momentum depends on both its speed and its size, it follows that being hit by a small car traveling at 15 miles per hour is likely to do less damage than a large one moving at the same speed.

But it is not only pedestrians who suffer from the presence of larger cars on the roads. Also at risk are all those riding in small cars. Being rear-ended by a 4,500-pound limousine is

likely to do far more damage to a subcompact, and its occu-
pants, than if two Honda Civics crash.

There is another fly in the ointment. Whenever something
happens to make a common activity less risky than people are
used to, they often adjust how they conduct that activity so
as to restore risk levels to their traditional, and higher, levels.
As we already saw, we can expect the driver of a large car—
knowing that it is safer—to drive it faster than he drove its
flimsier predecessor. In fact, plenty of evidence indicates that
people in large cars do drive faster than average, in effect
restoring their own risks to something like their original
levels. Leaving aside the fact that the driver of the heavier car
is frittering away most of his own gains in risk reduction by
driving faster, the salient point is that he is thereby making
his vehicle an even bigger menace to pedestrians and other
motorists than it would be at ordinary speeds. For such reasons, pedestrians, cyclists, and small-car owners are put at
greater risk with every heavy car that comes off the assembly
lines.

Ponder some different examples where, again, risk reduction fails to be beneficial to all. It is conventional wisdom that
both chlorinating and fluoridating tap water lower many
health and dental risks to most users of a public water system.
However, a small fraction of the population has strong allergic
sensitivities to fluoride or chloro-compounds.

Making houses more energy-efficient by eliminating sources
of drafts cuts down the risk of our dependence on foreign oil,
but such curtailment of air flow also dramatically augments
the presence of dust mites and molds in homes and offices.
Most people are not bothered by such critters, but, for a
minority of the population, they cause acute allergic attacks
and sometimes more serious long-term health conditions.

Everyone knows that reducing risk is not a cost-free

activity; we also need to understand that neither is it a particularly equitable one.

FOURTEENTH LAW:
NO INFORMATION MAY BE BETTER THAN SOME

Occasionally, no information is better than some—especially where your health is concerned. All of us over 30 can testify that one of the ways medicine has changed dramatically in our lifetimes is the explosion of diagnostic tests for various diseases and conditions. These days, it is not uncommon, even during a routine physical exam, for the doctor to order fifteen to twenty different blood tests in developing a patient's biochemical profile.

In part, the more extensive use of such tests is driven by the availability of newer and subtler diagnostic technologies. In equal measure, however, this explosion of testing reflects the litigation fears of physicians and, in some cases, the financial involvement of doctors in the labs that perform the tests.

From the patient's perspective, however, the key issue about all these tests is how far they serve his or her interests and health. There are a lot of thorny problems here. One of them arises because we are now in a position to test for many diseases and conditions that we know neither how to treat nor cure. It is a legitimate question to ask: Does a patient either want or need to know that she has some debilitating, untreatable condition? The answer is not clear-cut.

But suppose that the disease in question is treatable. In that case, surely tests seem relatively benign? Well, not necessarily, because some tests involve quite intrusive surgical procedures and considerable risk to the patient. Even where there is no invasive surgery, the test itself can sometimes harm the patient. (Ponder the fact that about 1 in every 10,000 persons who takes a coronary stress test dies from the procedure itself.)

Such tests, however, are not typical. Most involve no fatal risk to the patient. But there are other sorts of risks that patients run from such seemingly harmless tests. The principal risks are those of knowledge, error, and fear.

What I mean is this: Virtually every lab-conducted medical test involves sources of error. Test samples can be contaminated, or one sample can be confused with another. The report you get back from your doctor on a series of blood tests may belong to someone else. Particularly when the news is bad ("the test detected that you have AIDS, lupus, cancer,..."—you fill in the blank), such tests can produce fear, anxiety, and panic in their recipients.

These errors, although egregious enough, reflect sloppiness or carelessness and are, at least in principle, subject to tighter controls. A well-run lab will not permit them to occur, but there is another type of error that cannot be so readily managed. This arises from the nature of the testing process itself. Virtually every medical test designed to detect a disease or medical condition has a built-in margin of error. Its size varies from one test procedure to another, but it is often in the range of 1–5%, although sometimes it can be much greater than this. Error here means that, even when the test is properly conducted and there is no confusion among the samples, the test will sometimes indicate the presence of the disease *even when it is not there*. Such results are called false-positives, and they are the bane of the medical profession. Suppose a lab is using a test for a rare condition, one that has a 2% false-positive rate. (Remember that this means that the test will detect the disease in 2% of those who do not have it.) Among 1,000 tested for the disease and who do *not* have it, the test will report that about 20 persons have it. If, as we are supposing, the disease is rare (say it occurs in 0.1% of the population), it follows that the vast majority (here, 95%) of the people whom the tests report to have the disease will be misdiagnosed!

If this seems too abstract, consider a concrete example. Suppose that a woman (let us suppose her to be a white female, who has not recently had a blood transfusion and who does not take drugs and doesn't have sex with intravenous drug users) goes to her doctor and requests an AIDS test. Given her demographic profile, her risk of having AIDS is about 1 in 100,000. Even if the AIDS test were so good that it had a false-positive rate as low as 0.1% (and it is nothing like that good), this means that approximately 100 women from a cohort of 100,000 similar women will test positive for AIDS *even though only one of them has AIDS.* When we consider both the traumatizing effects of such reports on patients and their effects on future insurability, employability, and the like, it becomes clear that the false-positive problem is much more than just a technical flaw.

One lesson is clear: If your doctor ever reports that you tested positive for some rare disorder, you should be extremely skeptical. In all likelihood, the diagnosis itself will be a mistake. Knowing this, sophisticated physicians are very circumspect in their use of test results and in their subsequent consultations with patients. But not all doctors have the time or the savvy to treat test results with the skepticism that they often deserve.

FIFTEENTH LAW:
BEWARE THE POLITICALLY CORRECT RISK

Everyone—or at least every reader of women's magazines—has heard of the breast cancer epidemic, right? Well, there isn't one. What is true is that more women are being *diagnosed* with breast cancer than ever before. There are two simple reasons for this: (1) there are more women, especially elderly women, than ever before and (2) the techniques for diagnosis are more powerful than they have ever been. One factor that led some people to think that breast cancer itself must be on the rise was that the National Cancer Institute recently published an estimate that 1 in 8 women would acquire breast cancer sometime in their lives. Because earlier estimates (for example, from the American Cancer Society) had been about 1 in 9, this has been widely construed as indicating more than a 10% increase in the disease.

But the change here is not real; it's just an artifact of the statistics. The American Cancer Society estimate was based on the possibility of developing breast cancer *before* the age of 85. That remains, even with current figures, a chance of 1 in 9. The riskier figure from the National Cancer Institute, 1 in 8, was a projection of the risk of developing breast cancer *ever*, even after 85.

It may put this issue a little further into perspective to move away from talking about lifetime risks and to look at some concrete figures. For instance, a healthy woman at age 50 has about a 2% chance of getting breast cancer before she is 60. A healthy woman of 60 has about a 2% chance of getting breast cancer before she is 70. As these figures make clear, breast cancer is primarily a killer of the old, especially those 75 and older. Unlike AIDS or accidents, it claims relatively few younger victims.

In 1994, the U.S. government spent some $9,000 on research on breast cancer for *each* case of breast cancer that occurred during that year. This does *not* include the costs of treatment, diagnosis, or cure. These are costs of basic research. If we were to devote comparable sums to other killer diseases, such as heart disease, we should be spending $13 billion per year on heart disease research. We spend substantially less than half of that, and the same is true for other more common diseases. If one accepts the plausible idea that the money spent researching the cure for a disease ought to bear a pretty close relation to the number of people whom the disease harms or kills, one cannot resist the conclusion that breast cancer is receiving disproportionately large amounts of funding. To say as much publicly, however, is to invite abuse and invective from women's groups for whom breast cancer research has become symbolic of much larger political agendas.

Prostate cancer provides a useful point of comparison. A man is just as likely to get cancer of the prostate as a women is likely to develop breast cancer. Both forms of cancer exhibit roughly comparable survival rates, yet prostate cancer funding is poor compared to that for breast cancer.

Why the anomaly? The answer seems to be that strenuous lobbying efforts from women's health groups have created sufficient political pressure in Washington to push breast cancer to the top of our medical research agenda, even though the disease itself ranks well down the scale of major killers. Even among women, the risk of developing fatal heart disease, for instance, is much greater than the risk of dying from breast cancer.

SIXTEENTH LAW: REDUCING ONE RISK OFTEN EXACERBATES ANOTHER

Science and technology are remarkably efficient at identifying risks and at coming up with solutions to many of them. We are all aware that implementing such solutions can be very costly. (Witness the hundreds of billions of dollars being spent in the

WIRED TO WIN

In 1987, a man playing blackjack in Las Vegas was found to have a micro-computer wired to his calf. Via wires running to his shoes, he could keep track of the cards in play. The computer calculated his odds of winning and sent vibrations to a special receiver located in his jock strap!

United States to fight just one particular set of risks—airborne pollution.)

There is less public awareness that the dollar costs of reducing or eliminating a risk are only one part of the costs. In addition, we are discovering that almost every step we take to reduce one risk immediately introduces a new one, often of a completely unanticipated sort.

Ponder a couple of examples:

- Faced with the risk of deteriorating air quality in the 1960s and 1970s, the federal government encouraged Detroit to make more fuel-efficient vehicles. It turns out, of course, that one of the most effective ways to cut back on fuel emissions is to curtail fuel consumption by lightening the weight of the standard car. Small cars produce fewer carcinogens and less pollution than their bigger gas-guzzling cousins, but smaller cars are much riskier to drive; your chances of surviving a highway crash in a small car (say less than a ton) are less than half that of surviving a crash in a heavier car (2 tons or more). The trade-off here is between the prospects of a death from cancer at some remote point in the future and the heightened threat of a fatal crash now.

- The fuel crisis of the mid-1970s, along with a growing environmental consciousness, led many Americans to think that steps must be taken to make our homes and public buildings more energy-efficient, thereby lowering the risk of prematurely draining the planet's nonrenewable energy resources. To this end, homes were made more airtight so that heat was not needlessly escaping. Federal ventilation standards for the workplace and public buildings were also scaled back. That, in part, is why the air in airplanes and office buildings is now much staler than it used to be and why the frequency of "sick buildings" seems to be on the rise. The clear tradeoff here is that as structures become more airtight, the risks of all those airborne diseases to which we are prone—from the carcinogens in tobacco smoke and cooking oil to the smoke from our wood stoves and the germs from our office mate with flu—go up in direct proportion to the extent that we succeed in achieving energy savings as we seal up the places where we live and work.

If these examples strike you as out of the ordinary, think again. Comparable ones are all around us:

- Every time you take a prescription drug to cure some ailment, the medicine comes with a label chronicling possible side effects from using the medication. For a minority of the users of almost any medication, the cure can be far worse than the disease.

- Cities chlorinate drinking water to tackle the problem of waterborne diseases, but chlorine in water produces small amounts of chloroform, a human carcinogen, which may trigger cancer in anyone who drinks water from the tap.

- Older Americans are often advised to take aspirin to prevent strokes, but they are also warned about what it does to the stomach.

- In states like Florida that have introduced tough laws to combat the risks of drunk driving, there has been a significant increase in deaths among drunken bicyclists.

- We buy air bags for our vehicles to lower the risk of death and injury in front-to-rear crashes, but the velocity of inflation of the bags may produce forces that pose a mortal danger to young children riding in infant seats beside the driver (not to mention the risk of accidental inflation of the bags).

What these and dozens of similar examples show is that risk control always has a double price tag attached. In deciding whether to tackle a present risk, we must ask ourselves both what the direct costs are and what new risks we may be introducing. Sometimes, given the tradeoffs, it makes more sense to live with the risk than to tackle it.

SEVENTEENTH LAW: ERRING ON THE SIDE OF CAUTION MAY BE THE WORST THING TO DO

All of us grew up with the safety clichés of our time. We were told that one is "better safe than sorry" and that the wise person "errs on the side of caution." These bits of home wisdom have been incorporated into many of our official policies toward risk. Numerous federal agencies, for instance, work on the conservative theory that if a product or substance is possibly risky, then it should be banned or tightly regulated— at least until such time as its safety has been assured. New pharmaceuticals, for instance, cannot be sold in the United States until and unless their safety has been proven.

I have no quarrel with the prudent idea that when we *know* the relevant risks then the cautious approach, minimizing our risk exposure, is the best strategy. The trouble is that this attitude now permeates our thinking about all kinds of situations, even where the risks are unknown. If we think something *might* go wrong, but don't know the relevant odds, we are likewise apt to be wary. If we suspect, perhaps on the basis of anecdotal evidence, that something *might* be dangerous, we lean toward banning it.

In some cases, such aversion to risks whose danger levels are unknown backfires. Consider the classic case of the banning of DDT in 1972. The official reason for the ban was that DDT might pose (in the words of then-EPA chief William Ruckelshaus) "a carcinogenic risk." At the time, DDT was very widely used as an insecticide, and it had been largely credited with saving millions of lives from malaria and other insect-borne diseases.

Back in 1972 (as now), no one had robust evidence that DDT caused cancer in humans, but there was some basis for thinking that it might. Accordingly, erring on the side of caution, its sale and use in the United States were proscribed. A victory for prudence? Quite the reverse. Absent DDT, many farmers and others who needed to control insect outbreaks went over to using organophosphate insecticides (such as parathions). These, it later turned out, were hundreds and in some cases thousands of times more toxic to humans than the DDT that they replaced.

A similar example is the handling of the possible risks of saccharin. During the 1970s, several rodent studies suggested that massive doses of saccharin might cause bladder cancer in human beings. Throughout the 1980s, although the government's plan to ban the sugar substitute stalled in Congress, millions of Americans shied away from saccharin thinking that it *might* harm them. Although it is true that saccharin might be harmful, it is beyond dispute that getting the same sweetening power in the form of sugar is much more harmful. Obesity kills far, far more Americans than bladder cancer ever did.

The point is that it is often very difficult for us to decide, in any given case, what is the prudent thing to do. Because dangers potentially lurk everywhere, the only sensible strategy is to insist that dramatic actions ostensibly in the name of lowering risk must themselves be based on solid evidence rather than conjecture or hearsay (as in the banning of DDT or the Alar and saccharin scares). The idea that we can pre-emptively protect ourselves from possible dangers by banning them the moment we discover that they might be risky is a road paved with good intentions; like all such roads, however, it leads to unpleasant consequences.

This decade's "in" risk—global warming—is an excellent case in point. Scientists continue to dispute whether the release of carbon dioxide will drive up global temperatures and, if so, by how much. They likewise are unclear about whether the effects of a slightly warmer earth would be benign or malignant. Where such massive uncertainty exists, it is wholly unclear whether herculean efforts to stem CO_2 emissions (with all the foreseeable dislocations that would ensue) are putting us at greater or lesser risk than if we took no action.

Instead of erring on the side of caution, shouldn't we be seeking not to err at all?

EIGHTEENTH LAW: SCRUTINIZE THE NUMBERS

When someone wants to scare you about an activity that is not actually very scary, he can often find a way to describe the risk so that you will infer something more than is actually there. An interesting example is provided by the federal government's recent efforts to intimidate senior citizens into using condoms. Yes, that is what I said. The nosy folks at the National Institutes of Health have decided that too many elderly Americans have been engaging in unprotected sex. To change those habits, the feds have begun a (dis)information campaign. For instance, in January 1994, they voiced public concern that older Americans (that is, those over 50) are only 17% as likely to use a condom during sex as people in their 20s. The authorities want to see the situation change. Perhaps they should offer free condoms in seniors centers?

The government justified its targeting of seniors in its condom campaign by pointing out—which is true—that the proportion of those over 50 who get AIDS from *heterosexual* sex is higher than for any other age group in the population. What is one supposed to infer from such a statistic? If you don't read it

> **RISK GEOGRAPHY**
>
> A Russian man is 3 times more likely to commit suicide than a U.S. man.

carefully, you might think at first that it says that a lot of folks over 50 get AIDS from heterosexual intercourse. But of course it says nothing of the sort, for that would be patently false. What it asserts, rather, is that *if* a person over 50 does get AIDS, then he is more likely than a younger AIDS victim to have acquired it from the opposite sex. That should surprise no one, however, because the proportion of practicing homosexuals in the 50+ population is much smaller than among those under 30. This piece of information, as I first formulated it, is obviously meant to send seniors scurrying to have a discrete conversation with their local pharmacist, but the idea that the average American—least of all American seniors—is highly at risk for AIDS from typical heterosexual contacts is preposterous. (See the end of Chapter 3 for details.)

NINETEENTH LAW:
SOME PEOPLE ARE BEYOND HELP!

If, like me, you were to spend many of your idle moments pouring over columns of risk data and safety statistics, you would soon develop an eye for a species of risk that I call the mind-boggler. To be a mind-boggler, a statistic obviously must be unexpected and surprising, but many come in that category. The true mind-boggler is the one that is so absurd, so improbable, that you can't begin to get your brain around it.

For instance, ponder the fact that 2,000 Americans each year injure themselves on a child's balloon. These injuries are not the low-grade sort that you might get if, say, you stretched a balloon to its full length and then aimed it at some private body part. The injuries here are serious, requiring immediate emergency-room treatment. How does one do *that* with a balloon?

Here are a few of my other current risk favorites. I warn you that you need a well-honed sense of the absurd to appreciate some of them.

Annually, some 4,000 of us seriously injure ourselves on pillows. I recently tried to reproduce this one myself. The closest I could come was getting my neck caught in the zipper of the pillowcase. I didn't bother calling the emergency room, because I knew that their policy is to treat only the most acute types of zipper cases, involving hips and other parts well below the neck.

Another 3,000 people injure themselves on their room deodorizers. I bought two or three models to try them out. One is the liquid-in-a-bottle sort, with a pull-out wick. I reckon that maybe people try to swallow the wick assembly— perhaps on the theory that it can do double duty as a breath freshener. I couldn't figure out any other way to do it. I also bought one of those plug-in sort of deodorizers. It appeared to have no moving parts and was smooth plastic. I banged my head with it a few times but couldn't pretend even to myself that it hurt. Maybe people stick the electric prongs in their eyes? Or break a tooth chewing on the thing? It's beyond me.

Of course, people do not always tell the truth. Maybe they show up at the emergency room after coming to blows with a spouse or neighbor. Asked by the emergency-room nurse how they got that dislocated shoulder, they say whatever pops into their minds—something like, "My deodorizer did it."

Sometimes the mind-bogglers are of a different sort, arising from doubt about whether people really know what they are doing. For instance, what does one make of the fact that traffic police officers have more accidents per mile of driving than the average driver does? Or, speaking of police, that more cops are shot by other officers than by the crooks?

Most of the drowning deaths in the United States involve people who are in the water by accident rather than by design. We're talking here about thousands of fatalities every year. How, I ask myself, can *that* many people fall in the water?

We are routinely reminded about the importance of driving safely around children and the school buses carrying them. The mind-boggler is that a child embarking or disembarking a school bus is more likely to be run over by the school bus itself than by a passing motorist. Perhaps the real truth about why we make bus drivers turn on their blinking lights whenever they stop is not that it's so important to alert other drivers to the risks as it is crucial to remind the bus driver that she'd better be careful here because—in case she hasn't noticed—children are getting on and off her bus!

One of the worries that many married couples face at some time or other is the risk of an unwanted child. You probably thought that problem was solved 40 years ago with the invention of the birth-control pill. Well, maybe not. It turns out that, among fertile couples who firmly claim to want no other children, fully 10% of them are using *no* method of birth control. Maybe they think babies come from storks?

You say to yourself, someone is making this stuff up. Perhaps, but it is not me.

2

Jobs and Money: What You Didn't Learn in Economics 101

Many of the risks that worry us most represent threats to our life or our health, amply treated in later chapters of this book. Here, we are going to examine some of the risks to our pocketbook, to business, and to the investor.

If we are to believe the results of numerous studies of marital friction and breakups, most U.S. couples—and presumably singles, as well—worry intensely about money: Do they have enough? How can they acquire more? Will there be enough in the family kitty to send Pamela to Harvard or to buy that vacation cottage or to enjoy retirement? The issues are genuine enough, deeply tied up as they are with the American Dream.

But there is some reason to think that, like the weather, people worry about economic risks and problems much more than they *do* anything about them. Consider, for instance, that the average net worth of a married couple 65 or over (excluding the equity in their home) is about $56,000. This sum *might* cover 3 months in a nursing home for *one* of them. Younger couples are in even worse shape. U.S. Commerce Department figures indicate that the personal debt of the average U.S. household is about $75,000, while the total savings of that same family runs about $4,200. In sum, the average American family borrows about $18 for every $1 it saves. That family fortune in the cookie jar might cover about 6 to 7 weeks' worth of expenses for the family should they lose their jobs. Given how close most of us are living to the financial edge, it is especially worth knowing what the risks are that something might nudge us over that precipice.

GOING IN HOCK?

Risk that you will be seriously delinquent on your mortgage payments this year: 1 in 20.

Chance that your mortgage will one day be foreclosed: 1 in 8.

Odds that it will be foreclosed this year: about 1 in 100.

RISK GEOGRAPHY

City where you are least likely to own your own home: Newark, N.J. (77% are renters).

Risk that a white couple's application for a home mortgage will be turned down: 1 in 7. A black couple's application: 1 in 3.

Speaking of debt, the payments you make on your credit card, car loan, or draft from the finance company typically amount to almost 20% of your disposable income (and this is *apart* from payments on the mortgage on your home, if you have one).

A person is 8 times more likely to declare bankruptcy in Tennessee than in Hawaii.

BUILDING THE NEST EGG?

For years, it was the conventional wisdom among savvy investors that the best way of minimizing risk was to use the method called dollar-cost averaging. This strategy involves small and regular investments over a period of time rather than lump-sum commitments of capital. While it is true that you minimize your losses using dollar-cost averaging, recent studies have shown that, had you put all your money in the New York Stock Exchange at *any* specific point between 1926 and 1991, you would probably have made more money by the lump-sum method than by averaging.

Financial planners urge us to build up a hefty nest egg, independent of Social Security. How many of us are doing it? Well, ponder a pair of statistics. One of them is that if you are between 25 and 55, the odds are more than 50% that you have set aside *no* money for retirement.

The other telling figure is that, among U.S. workers in general, the odds that you are *not* covered by an employer pension plan is 65%. (An interesting exception to this pattern is government workers, whose odds of not being covered by a pension plan are a bare 8%.)

We Americans are generally a bit better about looking after our health than preparing for our old age. The odds that you don't have any form of health insurance are only about 14%, but if you're among the 86% who are now covered for heath care costs, you shouldn't be too complacent. Judging by experience from 1990 to 1995, you stand a chance of losing your health insurance coverage at any time.

For instance, in 1996, the risk that you could lose it (literally) tomorrow was about 1 in 10,000; that you could lose it in 1997, about 1 in 30.

ENDING UP IN THE POOR HOUSE

Strange as it might seem, poverty kills. In general, the poorer you are, the shorter your life span; the richer you are, the longer you live.

A very poor person (in the lowest 10% of income) will die about 10 years sooner than someone whose income puts him or her in the highest 10%.

Among the poor, poverty is responsible for more years of lost life due to premature death than smoking or heart disease or cancer. The elimination of poverty would do far more for public health and longevity than any other public health measure.

Major U.S. city in which you are most likely to be *both* poor *and* unemployed: Detroit.

RISK GEOGRAPHY

State with the lowest average annual wage: South Dakota ($18,000).

Chances that you are officially poor: 15%—meaning that you live at or below the government's definition of the poverty level. (For a family of four, the feds say you're poor if you make less than about $16,000 per year.) Here's how it breaks down in a bit more detail:

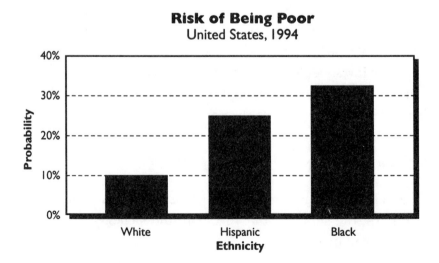

Risk of Being Poor
United States, 1994

Odds that you are now receiving some form of public assistance: 1 in 10.

Odds that you are homeless: 1 in 400.

Chances that a child living with its mother but not its father will be living below the poverty line: 47%.

> **RISK GEOGRAPHY**
>
> State where you are most likely to be living below the poverty line: Mississippi (roughly 1 in 4 persons). You're least likely to be that poor in Wyoming (1 in 12 persons).

EARNING YOUR WAY

People often think of poverty and unemployment in the same breath. The fact is that plenty of *working* people are officially impoverished. For instance, one-third of U.S. men aged 25–34 holding full-time jobs earn too little to lift a family of four above the poverty line.

> **RISK GEOGRAPHY**
>
> State with the highest average annual wage: New York ($32,000).

The chances that a working person will be poor are obviously even greater when they can find only part-time work. Women are twice as likely to be part-time employees as men are.

At the other end of the income scale, the risks are of a different sort, chiefly discrimination on the basis of sex or race. For instance, the odds that a senior manager of a *Fortune* 500

> **GETTING TO WORK**
>
> You probably spend about 22 minutes per day commuting to work.
>
> State with the slowest average commute to work: New York (29 minutes).
>
> State in which you're most likely to walk to work: Alaska (1 in 9 workers).

company is a woman are barely 1 in 20. The odds that a senior manager is black are about 1 in 30. Although more senior managers are women than black, employment statistics make clear that it is harder for a woman—white or black—to find her way into senior management than for a black man.

Although the gender gap shows up vividly when we look at figures on senior management, it has closed quite dramatically in many lines of work.

For instance, in 1994, women earned only 5–10% less than men in most professions. Interestingly, women mechanics and nurses make about 5% *more* than men with comparable qualifications.

Of course, having a job now is no guarantee of having one later. Although rates of unemployment vary with the business cycle, these patterns generally hold true among those in the workforce:

> ## RACE, EDUCATION, AND EARNINGS
>
> In 1994, the average college-educated black woman earned slightly more than white women with similar education.
>
> Among working men with a college education, whites and blacks are equally likely (about 30%) to be in managerial or executive positions.

- Men are at slightly greater risk of becoming unemployed than women.
- Blacks and Hispanics are twice as likely to be unemployed as whites.
- Those in the 16–19 age bracket are 3 times as likely to be unemployed as older workers.
- Among all the major industries, the lowest rates of unemployment are found among government workers; the highest rates are usually in construction.

Chances of losing your job this year: 3%. If you are a farm worker, the odds are more like 12%.

If you are unlucky enough to be unemployed, how tough life will be depends very much on where you live. For instance, unemployment benefits in Ohio are double those of Mississippi.

Several myts about the minimum wage pervade public debate about that issue. These data may lay some of them to rest:

RISK GEOGRAPHY

If you move your residence, the odds that you will move to Los Angeles: 1 in 20.

- Your odds of being paid at (or below) the minimum wage are only about 3%.
- The age group most likely to receive the minimum wage is 65+, who typically use their earnings to supplement their social security.
- A woman worker is twice as likely as a man to be paid at or below the minimum wage.

A recurrent worry for many American families is that the breadwinner may have to go out on strike, spiking the family income for weeks or months at a time. Such strikes, especially national ones, always get broad press and TV coverage, so much so that some Americans see them as a threat to our economy. In fact, American workers strike scarcely at all. The amount of time that the average worker spends out on strikes is 20 minutes per year. Because most of us work about 2,000 hours per year, loss of worker time directly due to strikes is about 0.01% per year.

In the past, trade unions were often blamed for strikes and other forms of industrial action on behalf of workers. Did the unions make a difference for their members? Well, ponder this: the average union member in 1994 earned about $7,000 more than the average nonunion worker.

The 1990s have become known as an era when employers—in the interests of being lean and mean—abandon traditional practices of preserving employee jobs and seek ways to cut numbers of employees to the bone. Critics of this practice often charge that it discourages employee loyalty, which it doubtless does. But such loyalty is often little more than a myth because, through most of this century, employees have jumped jobs much more often than employers have laid them off or fired them. Specifically, for every American fired from a job, there are four others who choose to leave.

Job mobility tends to be highest not among corporate executives, but among factory workers, 40% of whom will change jobs this year.

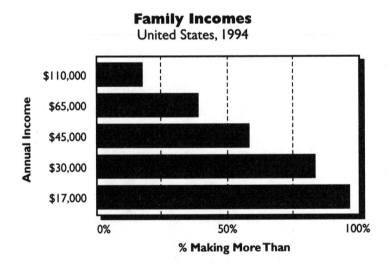

Family Incomes
United States, 1994

Slipping behind? Since the 1970s, wages of the average U.S. worker have barely kept pace with inflation, but that same worker's fringe benefits have been dramatically increasing since 1970. In fact, in 1994, the average U.S. worker received about $5 per hour in fringe benefits, over and above his or her salary. The average hourly wage itself was about $13, but the package came to about $18. (None of this explains, of course, why my car repair shop has the gall to bill me for "labor" of $70 per hour!)

Odds that your current job is more or less what you intended to do when you were young: 1 in 2.

Odds that you'll have to take a drug test if you apply for a job with a large company: 1 in 3.

Odds that if you smoke, you will be *not* be considered for a job for which you are otherwise qualified: 15%.

Odds that if you work, you receive a salary rather than an hourly wage: 40%.

RISK GEOGRAPHY

A worker in Alaska is 20 times more likely to receive a fatal injury at work than a worker in Connecticut.

The second most common cause of death on the job is assault from a coworker or client.

Odds that if you die at work, it will be as a homicide: 17%. You are 3 times more likely to receive a fatal injury off the job than at work, and you are almost twice as likely to receive a disabling injury *off* the job as on.

A taxi driver is 2 to 3 times more likely to be murdered on the job than a police officer.

Riskiest industry for injuries: meat packing.

HIGH-RISE, HIGH RISK

Fourteen workers died in accidents while constructing the Empire State Building (1930–31). Lest you think things have changed for the better, ponder the fact that today in New York City there is one construction death for every $300 million spent on construction.

Odds that an on-duty firefighter's meal will be interrupted: 3 in 5.

Mining and agriculture have long been, and remain, the major industries posing the greatest risk of death to workers.

THINKING OF STARTING A BUSINESS?

Chances that a business will go bankrupt this year: 1 in 5.

Odds that a *new* U.S. business will go bankrupt in the next decade: 2 to 1.

Percentage of new firms in high technology that fail before their fifth year: 60.

An established business is more likely to fail in Rhode Island than in any other state.

State in which a *new* business is most likely to fail: Washington. Least likely: Wyoming.

Estimated cost of the Savings and Loan bailout of the 1990s: $300–500 billion.

> ### GREMLINS IN THE COMPUTERS?
>
> During February 1988, Wells Fargo Bank issued clients' monthly equity loan account statements with this sales message inadvertently printed at the bottom:
>
> YOU OWE YOUR SOUL TO THE COMPANY STORE. WHY NOT OWE YOUR HOME TO WELLS FARGO? AN EQUITY ADVANTAGE ACCOUNT CAN HELP YOU SPEND WHAT WOULD HAVE BEEN YOUR CHILDREN'S INHERITANCE.

> ### HISTORY IN A BOX
>
> During the first three years of the Great Depression (1930–33), 1 in every 3 banks failed.

Percentage of bankrupt thrifts that failed because of white-collar crime: 70–80%.

Between 1983 and 1992, 10 times as many U.S. banks failed as in the previous decade.

The courts have ordered Exxon to pay $7.7 billion for the 1989 Valdez tanker spill. This fine amounts to about $700 per gallon spilled.

One of the chief risks facing the farmer, apart from weather, involves the selection of crops or livestock on which he or she is going to concentrate. Wrong decisions here can be terribly costly. A cattle rancher, for instance, currently receives 10 times more per pound of beef he sells now than his grandfather did in 1940. A chicken farmer receives only twice as much, and a peanut farmer gets barely half what he received in 1940.

If you own rental property, it's likely to be vacant about 7% of the time (14% in Alaska; only 4% in Connecticut).

PAYING UNCLE SAM
AND HIS FIFTY LESSER RELATIVES

If you're an average American, about 34% of your working day is spent earning enough money to pay your taxes. Put differently, each of us is donating about 4 months of labor per year to government. Fifty years ago, about 25% of Americans' income went for taxes.

> **RISK GEOGRAPHY**
>
> City with the highest combined city and county taxes: Washington, D.C.

Chances that if you call the Internal Revenue Service for tax assistance, no one will answer your call: 1 in 3.

Chances that your federal tax return will be audited this year: 1 in 70. If it is audited and you are found to owe back taxes, the average amount you will be set back is $350–400.

A state tax return in Utah is 10 times more likely to be audited than one in Hawaii.

Chances that you are eligible for some form of veterans' benefits: 1 in 3.

LIFESTYLES

Chances that you do not have

- a phone: 6%
- a TV: 2%
- a VCR: 20%
- a personal computer: 75%

The Asian Economic Miracle? Chances that a Japanese home does not have central heating: 80%. That it lacks a flush toilet: 60%.

Many people buy cellular telephones for their convenience and their cachet, often not realizing that, on average, they risk running up average phone bills of $2,000–$2,500 per year—over and above their regular telephone service.

Tempted, when you fly, to use that nifty telephone built into the back of the seat in front of you? Unless you read the fine print, you won't realize until too late that you're likely to be charged about 10-15 times more than the same calls would cost if placed from a residential phone. One hapless flyer ran up bills of $4,000 on a single flight from New York City to San Francisco.

Odds that you live in a mobile home: 1 in 15.

Age group most likely to live in a mobile home: 65+.

Number of years you are likely to spend at your current residence: 2. The chance that you will change your residence this year are about 40%.

Chances that your household owns mutual funds: 31%.

> **RELIGION AND CAPITALISM**
>
> Jews, Unitarians, and agnostics have the highest average household incomes in the United States. Hindus and Buddhists have the lowest.

The restaurateur's dream-come-true: The average American spends one-third of his or her food budget on meals away from home.

Only in America: On average, each of us spends more every year on legal and attorneys' fees than on health insurance.

Inflation takes its toll: Consumer goods that cost you $1 in 1970 cost about $4 in 1996.

The rich get richer...

- Chances that you drive a luxury car: 11%

while the poor get poorer...

- Chances that you have no vehicle: 13%

OTHER GAMES OF CHANCE

Not all the economic risks that we run are in the line of duty. Some of us have been known to wager on games of chance from time to time. Going to a casino is one way to guarantee that you will lose your money over the long run. (The typical casino makes about 5% on every bet made.) Still, those odds are much better than you will find in any of the state-run lotteries, where you are playing against odds massively stacked against you. When I say massively stacked, I don't simply mean that your odds of winning are small—that would be okay, considering that the pots to be won are massive. I mean, rather, that states conducting lotteries skim a much higher proportion off the top for themselves than any commercial casino would be permitted to claim as profit.

Gambling with friends tends to offer better odds, provided, that is, that your fellow gamers aren't shysters. Lest you think that crooked gamblers are a phenomenon of the past, realize that, according to experts, 1% of all playing cards sold in the United States are marked, whereas about 10% of dice used in noncasino crap games are crooked.

GENDER IN THE CASINO

A woman is twice as likely to play roulette or the slot machines as a man. Men are more likely to play craps. Poker and blackjack are the only casino games played by men and women in roughly equal proportions.

3

Sex, through the Eyes of a Risk Theorist

Many of us who lived through the 1960s recall it as a time when sex was unqualifiedly fun. (Remember *The Joy of Sex?*) In large measure, that heady attitude depended—in ways that many of the participants never quite realized—on technology having got the risks of sex largely under control. Before the 1950s, sex and promiscuity were associated with syphilis and gonorrhea, both crippling diseases. Antibiotics took care of them. Equally, sex was associated with unwanted pregnancies, and the pill eliminated that worry for most of the 1960s swingers. The prospect of risk-free sex not only changed a lot of people's attitudes but also their practices and lifestyles.

For better or worse, that carefree situation was not to last long. First, disturbing stories emerged about how taking the birth control pill could cause serious, sometimes fatal, cardiovascular events. Barely had people begun to adjust to this realization before AIDS and HIV arrived, dramatically upping the anxiety level for those playing loose and free on the singles scene. Here, as elsewhere, risk and people's perceptions of risk have done a great deal to determine the choices we make in life.

Curiously, the data we have about the magnitude of these two sex-related risks suggest that people's reactions have been out of proportion to the size of the risks themselves. The birth control pill, for instance, is far safer than most medications, especially for nonsmokers, and even for smokers, taking the pill remains much safer than enduring the risks of dying during pregnancy and childbirth. As for AIDS, it continues to decimate certain groups (chiefly homosexuals, intravenous drug users, and hemophiliacs), but the threat it poses to those who engage exclusively in heterosexual sex is extraordinarily small. (For the details, see later in this chapter.)

The fact is that there are plenty of other risks and dangers associated with sex apart from pregnancy, AIDS, and the pill. This chapter looks at some of them.

SEX: EARLY AND "UNHEALTHY"

The average U.S. woman has her first sexual intercourse about 5 years before she gets married. This means that the vast majority of young women lose their virginity as teenagers.

A young man of 18 is twice as likely (80%) as a woman of that age (41%) to have had premarital sex. (Given this disparity, one mildly wonders with whom the men are having it.)

Every parent's worst fear realized: Chances that a teenager's first sexual intercourse will take place in a car: 1 in 8.

One might guess that teenagers are frightened of getting pregnant. Apparently they don't see it that way, because barely 50% of sexually active teenagers use *any* form of birth control.

> **AND WE USED TO THINK IT WAS HEALTHY**
>
> Do you realize that Uncle Sam—specifically the federal Centers for Disease Control—considers unmarried women ages 14–21 who have sexual intercourse to be engaging in an "unhealthy behavior"? So, it's official: Premarital sex is a risk to your health. Judging by their actions, 61% of the relevant female population thinks otherwise.

Of those sexually active teenagers who do use some form of birth control, about half use condoms. This means that about ¾ of teenage sex is, as the government discretely likes to put it, "unprotected."

Given that the use of a condom cuts the risk of acquiring a sexually transmitted disease (STD) in half, it is no surprise that large numbers of teenagers acquire an STD at some time or other.

Chances that an American will get an STD this year: 1 in 20.

The most common STD is gonorrhea, which 1% of teenagers have at any given time. (It is 10 times more common than syphilis.)

Girls ages 10–14 are twice as likely to have gonorrhea as women over 30.

A young black teenager is 5,000% more likely to have gonorrhea than a white teenager.

CONTRACEPTION

On the subject of condoms, it appears that there is a lot of pooled ignorance out there. Even about how to use them. For instance, a recent British study discovered that 1 in 5 adult men do not know how to put a condom on!

Who trusts whom? Of the *married* men who use condoms during sex with their wives, 15% have already had vasectomies.

The U.S. government is very big on condoms. The feds both set standards for their performance and routinely exhort all of us—including those scarcely at sexual risk at all—to use them.

Prior to the invention of the condom in the seventeenth century (the inventor was an Englishman, one Mr. John Condom), the most common form of contraceptive was a vinegar-soaked sponge, inserted into the vagina prior to intercourse.

Roughly 1% of the population has an allergy to latex (which is made from the sap of a rubber tree). Special condoms are available for these folks. They don't work as well, but it beats abstinence.

The number of condoms that the average U.S. male uses each year: 11.

PUTTING CONDOMS THROUGH THE WRINGER

The tests for condoms are quite an ordeal. At the government's insistence, condom makers test the likelihood that their product will break by filling them with about 6 gallons of air, inflating them to roughly the size of a small weather balloon. If they don't burst at that size, they're considered safe.

Apart from breaking, however, condoms might leak. They are tested for leakage by filling them with 10 ounces of water and then running something shaped like a rolling pin over them to see whether they remain dry outside.

It is not clear exactly what 6 gallons of air and 10 ounces of water are meant to simulate. Perhaps the tests are designed merely to give your average guy an inferiority complex.

Oil-based lubricants cause condoms to break. Fewer than half the adult male population knows this fact. Equally most men don't realize that there is a big-time difference in effectiveness between latex and natural-membrane condoms.

Figure this one out if you can: Among sexually active women who dropped out of high school, the married ones are much more likely to use a condom during sex than the unmarried!

What the Pope doesn't want to know: among all U.S. women ages 15–44, those who use the "rhythm method" of contraception: 1%. Fully 60% of women in that age group use some other form of contraception. Catholics use contraceptives in the same proportions as the rest of the population.

A woman who uses a contraceptive sponge is 50% more likely to become pregnant if she has already had a child than if she is childless.

A woman is less likely to get urinary tract infections if her sexual partner uses a condom than if she uses a diaphragm or spermicide.

THE OLDEST PROFESSION

Proportion of adult men who have had sex with a female prostitute: ⅓.

Chances that a *middle-class* man in the United States will at some time go to a prostitute: 1 in 5.

Chances that a Thai girl of 15 will work as a prostitute before she is 30: 1 in 10.

It's not just in Bangkok: Chances that a middle-class U.S. girl or woman will work at some time as a prostitute: 1 in 12.

Only 1 in 3 prostitutes regrets her choice of work.

That may have something to do with the fact that the average annual earnings of a call girl (as opposed to a streetwalker) are about $50,000.

The majority of prostitutes of both sexes claim to have entered the field because they wanted to rather than because they were forced to.

Percentage of prostitutes who are streetwalkers: 20%.

Risk that a streetwalker will have to spend more than half an hour soliciting her next trick: 50%.

Chances that a prostitute will at some time be beaten by her pimp: 2 in 3.

One-quarter of adult male prostitutes began regular prostitution by the age of 13.

Half of female prostitutes began by the age of 14.

Roughly ⅓ of female prostitutes were sexually abused as children.

A woman in Nevada, where prostitution is legal, is 1,000 times more likely to be a prostitute than a woman in Nebraska.

CURIOUS FACTS ABOUT SEX

Who said there was design in nature? Man's capacity for multiple ejaculations decreases with age, beginning at about 20. Woman's ability to have multiple orgasms increases with age.

In the United States, a man is more than twice as likely to masturbate as a woman. A German woman is more than twice as likely to masturbate as her U.S. counterpart.

The risk of not getting it up increases with age. Specifically, studies show that the angle of a man's erect penis decreases with age.

> **EDUCATION AND SEX**
>
> Compared to women with only a high school education, highly educated women:
>
> - have twice as many sex partners
> - are more likely to participate in oral sex
> - are more likely to masturbate
> - are less likely to enjoy parenting

The World Health Organization estimates that there are about 100 million women worldwide who have undergone genital mutilation.

Odds that adultery is a crime in the state where you live: 40%.

Proportion of Americans who have committed adultery: ½.

Odds that sodomy (even between married couples) is a crime in your state: 50%.

Percentage of heterosexual couples who have practiced anal sex: 40%.

The average U.S. adult spends about $50 per year on pornography.

He or she views about four X-rated movies per year.

The average American has about 2,500 sexual fantasies per year. This works out to about 7 fantasies a day.

Chance that your lover fantasizes during sex with you: 80%.

Hope springs eternal? A man is 3 times more likely to sleep in the nude than a woman.

Which sex likes sex best? Well, a wife is 3 times more likely to refuse her husband's request for sex than vice versa. Similar evidence comes from a different quarter. Young, gay male couples have sex more often than young, heterosexual couples do. Young lesbian couples have sex less often than either gay or straight couples. All of which may suggest that men are keener on frequent sex than women are.

Perhaps it's habit-forming: Divorced adults are more likely to have sex than are single, never-married ones.

The cardiovascular strain from sex can be fatal. The individual especially at risk for this type of fatal event is the middle-aged man during intercourse with an illicit lover. (And no, this research was not sponsored by the Institute for the Preservation of Marital Fidelity.)

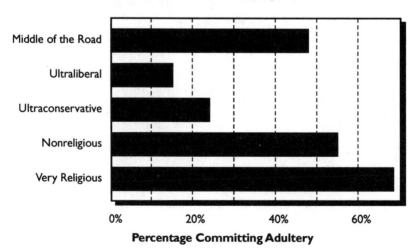

Fidelity and Ideology
Infidelity, Politics, and Religion

Women with migraine attacks tend to have more sexual fantasies than those who don't have migraine headaches. On the other hand, they masturbate less. (Maybe there's a connection here?)

Sex, like aspirin, has an analgesic effect on most aches and pains. (However, it has not yet been approved by the Food and Drug Administration for pain relief.)

The age of the onset of puberty has been declining throughout the industrialized world, as children enjoy better diets and fewer diseases. For a fraction of children, however, puberty comes very early indeed. Known as precocious puberty, this condition is exhibited by girls who reach puberty before age 8 and by boys pubescent before age 9. Chances that a child will have this condition: 1 in 10,000. The condition tends to be hereditary, especially among boys.

ACHING FOR SEX

Everyone has heard about the headache that precedes the act of intercourse (as in, "Darling, I've got a headache tonight"). Less well known, except in psychiatric circles, is the headache *caused* by sex. It is called coital cephalalgia (or, sometimes, orgasm headache) and occurs either during or immediately after orgasm. Roughly 1 in every 400 headaches is a coital headache. The headache can last for minutes or even hours and often resembles a migraine. It is thought to be triggered by the biochemical changes (especially in the circulatory system) that accompany orgasm. Men are more likely to have them than women.

Damned if you do, damned if you don't: A woman who has frequent sex, especially with different partners, increases her risk of cervical cancer. A woman who only rarely has sex increases her risk of ovarian cancer.

Kinsey's pioneering research in the 1950s suggested that as many as 10% of males might be homosexual. Since then, research has the numbers falling drastically.

Among sexually active adult Americans,

- 98% of the men had exclusively female sexual partners during the last year.
- 99% of the women had exclusively male partners during the last year.

A homosexual is 2 times more likely to become an alcoholic than a heterosexual.

AIDS RISK: CUTTING THROUGH THE HYSTERIA

What appears to be a simple question—"What is my risk of becoming an AIDS victim?"—turns out to be fiendishly complicated to answer. I will, however, make a stab at being clear about it—especially concerning the vexed issue of the risk of acquiring AIDS from heterosexual sex. All the numbers I will be using, some of which may surprise you, are derived from official figures on the incidence of AIDS and HIV published by the Centers for Disease Control.

The first thing to state up front is that we do not know how many people are now contracting AIDS. We have some good information about how many people are currently being *diagnosed* with the disease, but, because several years often pass between exposure and diagnosis, literally no one has up-to-date figures on exposure risks.

Even so, we can learn quite a lot from looking at diagnosis rates over the last few years, though even here we have to be careful. The truth is that the official medical definition of

AIDS has changed twice since 1986 (once in 1987 and again in 1993); each time, a *wider* definition of the disease replaced its narrower predecessor. These changes make a dramatic difference in how we count the numbers of those with AIDS. For instance, more than 70% of those diagnosed with AIDS in 1993 had symptoms that doctors would *not* have considered as AIDS 6 years earlier.

This broadening of the cluster of symptoms that are taken to characterize AIDS makes it necessary to be cautious when talking about time trends in the occurrence of the disease in the general population. When people say, as the media often do, that the AIDS epidemic is getting worse, they usually mean that the number of those diagnosed with AIDS is on the rise. The fact is that the numbers of those newly diagnosed with AIDS, as it was *originally* understood, has been steadily declining since 1990–91. What has not been falling dramatically is the total pool of persons newly diagnosed with AIDS—under the broadened definition. This number, according to the Centers for Disease Control, is about 100,000 victims per year.

It is that number that leads to the widely publicized risk figure that the average American has a *1 in 2,500* risk of acquiring AIDS this year. (If you divide the U.S. population by the annual number of new victims, this number simply falls out as the composite risk.)

Such a risk is obviously serious, especially given the fatality rate from AIDS. It is roughly twice the risk of being an auto fatality this year. But whenever we deal with risks at this level of aggregation, we are in grave danger of being mislead.

To see why, let us break down the risk more specifically. Suppose we want to calculate the risk of a typical white female acquiring AIDS. We can begin by asking: What is the risk that a woman will get (that is, be diagnosed with) AIDS this year? Because men in general are much more at risk for AIDS than women in general (80% of new AIDS cases are men), we can bring the risk down to about *1 in 10,000* for females.

As it turns out, black and Hispanic women are much more likely to get AIDS than white women. So, if you are white and female, your chances of getting AIDS are about *1 in 20,000*. This level of risk is not low, but it is only ⅛ of what it seemed at first glance.

But we're still not where we want to be because we want to find out the risk of acquiring AIDS for the *typical* white female. Many women who get AIDS acquire it by sharing needles during drug use. So we can ask: "What is the risk of a white woman who does not inject drugs getting AIDS?" The answer here is a risk of about *1 in 44,000*. We halved the risk yet again. Suppose, like most white females, she also has not had a blood transfusion. The risk is now about *1 in 50,000*.

All this explains why it is true that, if a white women has AIDS, she probably did *not* acquire it through sexual contact.

So far, we've not yet said anything about this woman's sex life, which appears to preoccupy the public health experts. Let's begin to factor that in. Suppose that our hypothetical typical white female does not have sex with intravenous drug users. In that case, her risk of acquiring AIDS this year is about *1 in 80,000*—roughly the same risk of dying this year from choking to death. Suppose, furthermore, that she does not sleep with bisexual males. Now the risk hovers around *1 in 103,000*.

Finally, let us imagine that she avoids sex with hemophiliacs or other recipients of blood transfusions. Her risk level now is around *1 in 120,000*. This degree of risk is quite remote; it's about on the same level as dying while riding your bicycle this year.

If questionnaire research is to be believed, millions of typical white women—especially unmarried ones—now rank their fear of contracting AIDS very high. They also indicate in overwhelming numbers that they have changed their lifestyles and love styles out of anxiety about AIDS. Well, if you are deeply risk-averse, I suppose that such changes make sense, but we have plenty of evidence indicating that these same women still drive cars, ride bikes, and do dozens of other things that are much, much riskier than having sex—even unprotected sex—with a heterosexual man. Under specifiable circumstances (and I do not mean celibacy or even monogamy), the threat that heterosexual sex will lead to AIDS is very low.

Incidentally, a comparable calculation for the typical white man (who doesn't shoot drugs or go to bed with women who do, doesn't get blood transfusions, and so forth) shows that his chances of getting AIDS this year are about *1 in 250,000*—roughly the same as dying in an airplane crash. In fact, since the beginning of the AIDS epidemic, fewer than 1,100 white men have died in the United States of AIDS as a result of heterosexual contact with nondrug users. An additional 600 have acquired AIDS but are still alive. Millions of white, American heterosexual males—most of whom are scarcely at risk at all—have been browbeaten into using condoms by the patronizing guardians of public health, who think the public is too stupid to have the real risks of AIDS explained to them.

If you are what I've been calling the typical white woman or man, you ought to find these numbers reassuring. The flip side of that coin, however, is that if you are not typical you may be highly at risk for AIDS. If you shoot drugs or are intimate with those who do, if you have sex with bisexuals or homosexuals, or if you frequently draw on the public blood supply, then every precaution you can imagine is probably called for.

The approximate risks that I have calculated here tell the average reader what he or she wants to know most about the AIDS epidemic; namely, the risk that they will get AIDS from sexual activity. Federal health authorities go to great pains *not* to circulate such information to the general public. It is hard to resist the conjecture that the feds' reluctance to promulgate such information stems from a fear that many people would lower their guard if they realized how nonrisky their own behavior was or, perhaps, they fear that the general public might oppose funding AIDS research and treatment programs if they realized that AIDS was principally an affliction of male homosexuals and drug addicts. Whatever the motives for such official obfuscation, people have a right to know what their own risk exposure is, however politically incorrect the facts about that exposure may be.

Speaking of general ignorance about these matters, surveys indicate that 17% of Americans believe that you can acquire AIDS by using a public toilet, while 27% believe that you can get it by being sneezed on by someone with AIDS.

Risk that you are HIV+: 1 in 250.

One of every $9 spent on medical research in the United States goes to HIV-positive–related activities.

Percentage of U.S. AIDS cases that were acquired via

- heterosexual sex: 6%
- drug use: 22%
- blood transfusions: 2%

During the 1980s, more than half the hemophiliacs in the United States were infected with HIV via blood transfusions.

Odds that you have a close friend or relative with AIDS: 19%.

Proportion of the population that has been tested for the presence of HIV antibodies: ⅓.

4

Eat, Drink, and Be Wary

There was a time when food was considered safe so long as the royal taster was still alive an hour after sampling it. Times have changed, but the paranoia remains. If food isn't contaminated, it's adulterated, full of pesticide residues, badly inspected, and laden with carcinogens, fats, calories, and other nasty stuff that take a lot longer than an hour to show up. What was once a pleasure limited to royalty for economic reasons—eating a hearty and delicious meal— is now denied to almost everyone for very different reasons, chiefly having to do with guilt about getting (or being) fat and anxiety about what the unseen stuff in our food or drink might be doing to us. The fact, and it is a well-documented fact, that food is mightily safer now than it ever has been does not seem to relieve our fretting about food. As this chapter will show, for all the improvements in food hygiene and diet, the dangers are still there. Testimony to some of those dangers can be seen in the statistic that some 9,000 Americans die each year from food poisoning alone.

The wonder is not that food sometimes harms us but that our diet is not killing more of us. Ponder a few numbers: The average person eats about 70,000 meals in a lifetime. That amounts to some 50 tons of food and about 10,000 gallons of liquid. (The amount of domestic waste you will generate in your lifetime is about 150,000 pounds; that is, each of us generates about 1,000 times his or her body weight in wastes.) The people in a small city (250,000) the size of Corpus Christi, Texas, or Norfolk, Virginia, consume enough food in their lifetimes to feed the entire world for a day. In principle, any of the food we consume might be dangerous; the liquids might be toxic. Most of the food we eat passes through dozens of hands (some of them doubtless contaminated) and numerous processes between point of origin and our palate. Medical historians say that the diet of our ancestors was the single biggest threat to their health. Only recently have we begun to understand what many of those threats are.

The average meal is digested in 2 to 4 hours; however, foods containing cellulose (such as lettuce and spinach) remain in the stomach for as long as 24 hours.

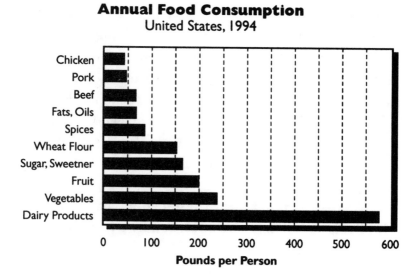

Annual Food Consumption
United States, 1994

HISTORY IN A BOX

During the Revolutionary War, 1 in 8 American seamen died each year from diseases related to shipboard diets. By 1900, the risk had fallen to 1 in 200. (Incidentally, more sailors died from bad diets during the first century of the Republic than died from *all* the wars of the period.)

The usual airline lunch or dinner contains less than 900 calories.

Believe it or not: Food served on U.S. airlines is regularly inspected by the Food and Drug Administration.

Odds that you'll have no fresh fruit at home this week: 21%. No fresh vegetables: 14%. No meat: 7%.

State where you are most likely to be undernourished: Mississippi.

If you regularly go without food for intervals of 15 hours or more (for example, by skipping breakfast), you increase your risk of gallstones.

Beta-carotene, especially when consumed naturally in foods rather than as a dietary supplement, appears to lower the risk of heart attack and of certain types of skin cancer—except in smokers.

Certain foods cause cavities because they temporarily alter the acidic concentration in the mouth, which in turn can destroy tooth enamel. Here are some culprits that rate especially high on the acid-producing scale (in *increasing* order of threat, reading down the list):

apple juice	lollipops	pies
orange juice	dates	sour balls
raisins	sweetened cereal	donuts
cakes	bread and jam	

Archaeological evidence indicates that Europeans in the Middle Ages had barely ⅙ the number of cavities of modern humans. On the other hand, the older ones (30+) had only about half their teeth remaining.

By the time you are 70, you'll have barely half the taste buds you had when you were 30.

Chance that a woman has food cravings: 95%; a man: 70%.

Every meat and poultry plant in the United States undergoes round-the-clock scrutiny from federal inspectors.

Percentage of U.S. cattle that have been treated with an estrogen-type growth hormone: 90% This worries some folks. It probably shouldn't, because the amount of residual estrogen in a normal serving of beefsteak is less than a millionth the amount of estrogen produced *each day* by a pregnant woman.

The average adult produces about 1.5 pints of gas per day—more if he or she is eating a high-fiber diet. So-called gas pains have little or nothing to do with the *quantity* of gas in the abdomen. In certain people, even small quantities of gas can produce discomfort.

Some beans produce more gas than others. The worst offender, ounce for ounce, is the soybean. Black beans and pinto beans are also very potent. According to experts who study these things (and what a thankless job they have), lima beans are among the weakest gas producers.

Odds that your next meal will be from McDonald's: 1 in 8.

Thinking of becoming a vegan? Finding replacements for dietary protein in meat is a snap. More challenging is the risk of iron deficiency (you'll need to consume about

8 pounds of broccoli or its equivalent daily to meet the minimum daily requirements) and lack of vitamin D.

According to the Centers for Disease Control, babies fed a vegan diet are slower to mature than meat-eaters; that is, they take longer to reach full size.

A woman is twice as likely to have mouth ulcers—caused by various foods—as a man.

Remember Mom's advice that eating *raw* vegetables was good for you? Not always:

- Raw lima beans contain toxic levels of cyanide.
- Raw red beans can cause acute gastroenteritis.

Solid waste disposal: The average American produces about 4–5 ounces of stool daily. The average rural African produces about 1 pound daily. For the African, that is about 12 tons of solid wastes over a lifetime.

WHEN FOOD CAN KILL

The most crucial factor involved in food poisoning is temperature control—either the temperature at which the food was kept after cooking or the temperatures of preparation and cooking. Frequently, food is cooked too far in advance of consumption; on other occasions, it is kept at room temperature for too long. Both factors are more common causes of food poisoning than food contamination is.

It is very difficult to tell how common food poisoning really is because the milder cases go unreported to doctors or public health officials. In fact, experts estimate that there are 30–150 mild cases of food poisoning for every 1 officially reported. If these estimates are right, each of us probably has several mild cases each year.

Sources of Food Contamination

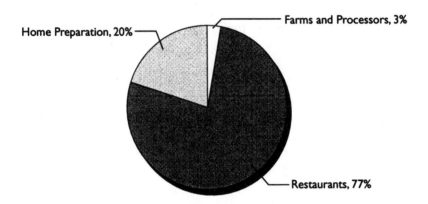

Home Preparation, 20%

Farms and Processors, 3%

Restaurants, 77%

Odds that you will get some serious form of food poisoning this year: 1 in 25.

Bacterial agents appear to be the cause of food poisoning incidents about 3 times as often as chemical contamination.

The most common source of botulism in the United States is home-preserved vegetables. In Italy and Spain, the chief culprit is home-preserved meats and sausages. The global fatality rate for botulism is about 10%.

Within the last few years, the most dangerous place in the world for botulism outbreaks has been Poland.

Meat is the food most commonly responsible for food poisoning, followed closely by fish and shellfish.

Leaving aside raw shellfish, the odds that you will die this year from eating seafood are about 1 in 5 million.

Irradiation of chicken meat can kill more than 99% of the *Salmonella* organisms that it may carry.

Raw eggs can be contaminated with *Salmonella*. Evidence suggests that roughly 1 in 10,000 eggs is so infected; however, cooking the egg well kills the bacteria. Provided cooked eggs are either refrigerated or eaten within 2 hours of cooking, they are quite safe.

According to a Minnesota study, you are much more likely to get food poisoning at a Mexican restaurant or at a deli than at an Italian restaurant.

The body's most potent defense against gastrointestinal infections caused by biological contaminants in foodstuffs is the highly acidic character of intestinal juices. Those who frequently take antacids, as well as many older people whose systems produce too little stomach acid, are at heightened risk for disease from such agents.

CANCER AND DIET

The food we eat accounts for about one-third of all fatal cancers, possibly more. In part, this is because virtually everything we consume contains carcinogens. Most of these carcinogens occur naturally; that is, they come in food in its natural state or arise from the cooking and preparation process. A few of these carcinogens come from food additives, animal drugs, and pesticide residues.

Experts offer the following calculation as a way of vividly comparing the sorts of cancer risks from the food we eat. If you were to eat a diet completely free of *all* artificial carcinogens, the lifetime risk that you will die of cancer from your diet would be 6.6%. If, however, you eat the way most of us do, consuming both natural and artificial carcinogens, your lifetime risk of dying from what you eat is 6.7%.

This breaks down as follows:

Lifetime Risk of Cancer Death	Category
6.59%	Traditional food
0.07%	Spices and flavorings
0.01%	Indirect additives
<0.01%	Pesticides and contaminants
<0.01%	Animal drugs
<0.01%	Food preparation

What these figures make absolutely clear is that the principal killer in the food we eat is the food itself—not the additives nor the residues, which get so much public attention. But how, you ask, could food itself cause cancer? We don't know yet, but toxicologists have established this much: that the bulk of the carcinogens we ingest when we eat come from *naturally occurring carcinogens*. Fish, most vegetables, many

A MAP THROUGH THE DIET AND CANCER MAZE

There are well-designed medical studies that appear to support *each* of these generalizations:

- Consumption of fat increases the risk of getting colorectal cancer and pancreatic cancer.

- Alcohol consumption increases the probability of rectal and colon cancers, as well as cancers of the esophagus, the larynx, and the breast.

- Heavy consumption of grains (especially corn and wheat) creates a higher risk of getting esophageal and stomach cancer.

- Eating cereal though reduces the risk of getting bowel cancer.

- Vegetables and fiber reduce the risk of getting colon and rectal cancers, whereas meat and fat increases those risks.

- Fish lowers the risk of getting cervical cancer.

fruits, and most spices consist of naturally occurring chemicals that are known carcinogens. (When administered in massive doses to mice, many chemicals that occur naturally in foods produce tumors, the customary test for carcinogenicity.) All the major organizations concerned with cancer control and prevention—including the National Cancer Institute, the American Cancer Society, and the U.S. Department of Health and Human Services—acknowledge that the overwhelming source of carcinogens in our diet is natural. For reasons that remain obscure, most Americans continue to believe that eating a "natural" diet—free of trace pesticides and other

THE UBIQUITY OF CARCINOGENS

The following substances all contain substances known to cause cancer in laboratory rats:

Substance	Carcinogen
wine	ethyl alcohol
beer	ethyl alcohol, furfural, urethane
air in home	formaldehyde, benzene
lettuce	caffeic acid
apple	caffeic acid
pear	caffeic acid
coffee	caffeic acid, hydroquinone, catechol, furfural
potato	caffeic acid
basil	estragole
diet cola	saccharin
peanut butter	aflatoxin
bacon	diethylnitrosamine
white bread	furfural
tap water	chloroform

CHANCE THAT PRODUCE WILL SHOW PESTICIDE TRACES	
Apples	97%
Celery	93%
Peaches	91%
Oranges, potatoes	79%
Grapes	75%
Bananas	61%
Broccoli	25%

Fewer than 2% of the detected residues exceeded levels permitted by the Environmental Protection Agency.

chemical residues—will eliminate or drastically curtail cancer risk from diet.

If, despite this, you're still worried about pesticide residues, you can avoid many of those in meat by cutting off the fat prior to cooking. Also, avoid eating internal organs such as liver and kidney, where these chemicals are apt to accumulate.

Eating large quantities of fruits and vegetables cuts your dietary cancer risk by about 50%, compared to those people who eat few of them.

Each year, the average American consumes about 20 pounds of preservatives, sweeteners, colorings, flavorings, and other chemical additives.

Each year, the Department of Agriculture performs more than 1 million tests on food for chemical and pesticide residues. During the last two decades, they have found no evidence of someone suffering serious health effects from residues on meat or poultry.

FIGHTING FAT

Number of U.S. adults who are fat (that is, more than 20% over the ideal body weight): 60 million.

According to the National Academy of Sciences, 35% of U.S. women 20+ are fat; 31% of men 20+ are.

Odds that you will start a diet this year: 20%.

In 1977, the Food and Drug Administration proposed a ban on saccharin—an artificial sweetener —on the grounds that it posed a significant risk of bladder cancer. The evidence then available suggested a lifetime risk of getting bladder cancer from saccharin of about 1 in 100,000. (As *lifetime* risks go, this is incredibly small.) What the FDA did not factor into its calculations was the fact that

> **RISK FACTORS FOR BEING FAT**
>
> You are at greater risk of being obese if you are:
>
> • older
>
> • female
>
> • black (among women)
>
> • poor (among women)
>
> • born into a family with a history of obesity

weight gain caused by eating sugar—instead of its substitute—is 100 times more likely to kill you than saccharin. Congress soon thereafter passed a special bill, exempting saccharin from FDA regulation.

In the last decade or so, the sweetener aspartame has been displacing saccharin as the sweetener of choice. Although not known to have carcinogenic properties, this sweetener does produce serious health effects in about 1 in 15,000 Americans.

Losing the Battle of the Bulge: Those who both begin and persevere with a weight loss program generally lose about 10% of their body weight. Within 1 year, they regain two-thirds of their loss. Within 5 years, almost all are back to their initial weight or higher. Does that mean they were wasting their time? Not necessarily, for there is no reason to suppose that, had they not dieted, they would have maintained their base weight. Maintaining your weight is, after all, better than increasing it.

Ever noticed how fatter people tend to be more gregarious and sociable than their skinny counterparts? There may be a natural explanation for this old cliché. If one has a meal alone, one eats only about two-thirds as much as when one has a meal with a companion. This would lead us to expect that loners would be skinnier than normal, whereas those who thrive on the company of their fellows would tend toward the fat.

How can we be eating a diet lower in fat and still putting on weight? The question is intriguing but the answer is simple arithmetic. Comparing figures from 1975 to 1990, it is clear that the average American is eating foods with a smaller proportion of fat than ever before (32% of our calories came from fat in 1990, whereas 34% were fat calories in 1978). The explanation of the weight gain: We're eating about 200 *more* calories daily now than we were then. While the *proportion* of fat calories has shrunk modestly, the *quantity* of fat calories consumed has actually increased.

The average *Playboy* centerfold weighs about 15% less than the average U.S. woman of the same height and age.

Large bones can add no more than about 10 pounds to your weight.

50% more C-cup brassieres are sold in the United States now than a decade ago.

10% of fat people reach age 80; 25% of thin people do. The details: fat people are more likely than those of normal weight to die of

- appendicitis
- cardiovascular disease
- strokes
- pneumonia
- kidney disease
- endometrial cancer
- postmenopausal breast cancer

The health picture is not all bleak for the overweight. One compensation: Obesity appears to *reduce* the risk of premenopausal breast cancer.

RISK GEOGRAPHY

State with the largest proportion of fat women: Michigan (29%) The smallest proportion: Colorado (18%).

If neither of a child's parents is overweight, his or her risk of being overweight is about 10%. If both parents are overweight, the risk increases to 80%.

The overweight and the obese are twice as likely to develop carpal tunnel syndrome from repetitive activities as those of slender or medium build.

A healthy woman has twice the body fat of a man.

Most extremely fat (40% over ideal weight) women who are now married were already extremely fat when they got married.

Among teenage girls, binge eating is relatively common. Many eat 4 times as much on a Saturday or Sunday as on any other day of the week.

A boon to health? Low-fat foods have a higher potential for bacterial contamination than their traditional fatty counterparts. This occurs chiefly because low-fat food tends to have a higher water content and is thereby more susceptible to microbe growth.

THINK YOU HAVE FOOD ALLERGIES?

Likelihood that you *think* you have some food allergy or intolerance: 1 in 4. I put it that way because when, in lab studies, people unknowingly consume the foods to which they think they are allergic, only about 2% of the population exhibits the allergy.

It's a different story where children are concerned; about 6% of them have food allergies.

Many people believe that the flavor enhancer monosodium glutamate, or MSG, makes them ill or produces an allergic reaction. However, when test subjects were unknowingly fed MSG over a period of 5 days, they did not report a high level of unpleasant reactions.

What food are you most likely to be allergic to? Nuts.

Chances that you have a fish or shellfish allergy: 1 in 1,000.

Chances that you are allergic to some food *additive* or other: 1 in 1,000.

It's widely known that some babies are allergic to cow's milk. That is one reason why breast-feeding is in fashion. What few parents realize is that some babies are allergic to their mother's milk—or, rather, to foods their mother

---

FOOD ALLERGIES

Here are the foods generally acknowledged to produce the most frequent allergic reactions:

Beans	Eggs	Soybeans
Berries	Fish	Sugar (cane and beet)
Booze	Milk	Tomatoes
Chocolate	Nuts (especially peanuts)	Wheat
Citrus fruits	Peas	Wine
Colas	Pork	Yeast
Corn		

Milk (Lactose) Allergies
by Ethnic Group

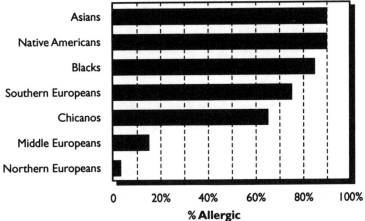

consumes and that then show up as trace antigens in her milk. The most common food that precipitates this problem in hypersensitive infants: cow's milk!

WHAT YOU DON'T WANT TO KNOW ABOUT WHAT'S IN YOUR FOOD

A recent Canadian study found the following sorts of contaminants in commercially produced foodstuffs: glass, wood splinters, stones, screws, needles, metal filings, sand, oil, paint chips, mice, worms, mites, mold, slugs, insect and mammal droppings, and cigarette butts.

Little attention is paid to one of the main ways in which contaminants are added to foods—cooking utensils. More than half of all cookware is made of aluminum. Some aluminum undoubtedly leaches into food, but this probably poses no problems. Aluminum is, after oxygen and silicon, the most common material in the earth's crust. Accordingly, every bit

---

WHEN ENOUGH IS ENOUGH

It falls to the experts at the Food and Drug Administration to decide how much contamination is to be allowed in foods sold for human consumption. That's right, I said "how much." It would be impossible to produce food that had no contaminants whatever. Here are some of the FDA guidelines for maximum permissible levels of certain "impurities":

Brussels sprouts	10 aphids per ounce
Shelled peanuts	1 insect per 5 pounds
Golden raisins	4 fly eggs per ounce
Tomato juice	3 fly eggs per ounce
Whole peppercorns	1% mammalian excreta
Popcorn	2 rodent hairs per pound
Fig paste	4 insect heads per ounce
Peanut butter	9 insect fragments per ounce
Canned mushrooms	5 maggots per ounce

It's quite a facer to realize that up to 1 in every 100 peppercorns we grind over our food could be a rat turd.

---

of food raised in the soil contains aluminum. So do most antacids and buffered aspirins. A few studies have found a link between high levels of aluminum in one's diet and Alzheimer's disease; other studies rebut this linkage.

As nonstick surfaces on pots and pans age, bits and pieces of this surface chip off, sometimes into food. They are chemically inert and, if ingested, simply pass through the body. Stainless steel can also leach into foods, but there is no evidence that it is harmful either.

It is a different story with uncoated copper cookware. Ingested in sufficient quantities, it can cause severe stomach upsets. Cast-iron pots leach significant amounts of iron into food, generally harmlessly.

GOOD TO THE LAST DROP?

Caffeine is the most widely used stimulant drug in the world. More than fifty different plants, apart from the coffee plant, contain this drug. Its effects are similar to those of amphetamines.

Researchers claim that symptoms of caffeine dependency develop in people who consume as little as 2½ cups of coffee (or its equivalent) daily. Heavy coffee (or tea) drinking often causes

- insomnia
- heart palpitations
- headaches

It can also cause nausea, constipation, and cardiac arrhythmias. Unfortunately, many of the same symptoms accompany caffeine withdrawal.

CAFFEINE EQUIVALENTS

Here are the amounts of various foodstuffs you would have to consume to get the amount of caffeine in 1 cup of drip-brewed coffee:

instant coffee	1.4 cups
tea	2 cups
Mountain Dew	2 12-ounce cans
Coca-Cola	2.2 12-ounce cans
Dr. Pepper	2.4 12-ounce cans
Pepsi-Cola	2.9 12-ounce cans
dark chocolate	5 ounces
milk chocolate	17 ounces
cocoa	20 cups
decaffeinated coffee	25 cups
No-Doz	1 tablet

"Decaffeinated" coffee still has 4% as much caffeine as ordinary coffee.

Young women who drink 3 or more cups of coffee per day are 25% less likely to conceive in a given month than women who drink much less or none.

Myths die hard: In 1980, the Food and Drug Administration issued an advisory to pregnant women to avoid coffee because it might produce birth defects. Although no credible evidence has ever emerged that would bear out this fear, many mothers-to-be continue to believe it.

If that is the good news about coffee and pregnancy, the downside is that, according to recent studies, the possibility of miscarriage is increased by caffeine intake during pregnancy.

There also appears to be a *weak* link between caffeine consumption and reduced fertility.

"PURE" WATER?

Chances that the next batch of bottled water you buy will be nothing more than bottled tap water: 1 in 4.

Speaking of tap water, the following known or suspected carcinogens were found in the drinking water of New Orleans:

chloroform	40 parts per trillion
ether	130 parts per trillion
dichlorobenzene	1,000 parts per trillion

Many other American cities would exhibit a similar profile.

When chlorine is added to tap water to kill bacteria, it produces a gas—chloroform—that remains in the water.

Scientists' estimate that your lifetime odds of getting fatal cancer from the chloroform in tap water: 1 in 100,000.

Except in a few states, bottled water is required to satisfy no purity standards beyond those imposed on tap water. Not only is bottled water not necessarily safer, it has never been shown to have health benefits over ordinary grade U.S. tap water.

Permissible levels of bacteria in bottled water are a generous 500,000 bacteria per liter. You'll be relieved to know that if it is more than that, the water cannot be sold.

In general, carbonated versions of bottled water are safer than the noncarbonated ones, because the carbonation lowers the pH, killing off many bacteria that would otherwise survive in the water.

Chlorination of water is very effective against bacteria; it is less effective against viruses and parasites in the water.

THE DEMON DRINK

Ethyl alcohol—the key ingredient in all alcoholic beverages— is both a carcinogen (it causes cancer) *and* a teratogen (it causes birth defects).

Odds that you are an alcoholic: 1 in 25.

An alcoholic is likely to die about 10 years younger than a moderate drinker or nondrinker.

Among drivers between 20 and 25 involved in fatal accidents, roughly half had been drinking. Among those 65 and over, the percentage of drunk drivers in driving fatalities is less than 10%. Some say this difference is because older people drink much less than younger ones. While there is some truth to that, my hunch is that many of the chronic

drunk drivers have already done themselves in
(or had their licenses permanently removed) well before
reaching 65.

Percentage of high school students who have been in a car
during the last month with a drunk driver: 35%.

The average Frenchman
drinks about 80% more
alcohol than his U.S.
counterpart.

> **RISK GEOGRAPHY**
>
> The state where a person you
> meet randomly on the street
> is most likely to be drunk:
> Nevada.

Black and white men have
physiologies that allow them
to digest alcohol more quickly than women, Native Americans, and Japanese. This means that, drink for drink, the
latter have more alcohol in their bloodstream than white
and black males do.

The average American or European adult consumes about
10% of his or her calories in the form of alcohol.

> **RISK GEOGRAPHY**
>
> No surprises here—state
> where it is hardest to get a
> drink: Utah.

Men are most likely to be
heavy drinkers between ages
21 and 34; women between
ages 21 and 49. (It is probably not politically correct to
note that these are also the
principal child-rearing years for most adults.)

The skeletons abound: Odds that you have an alcoholic or
problem drinker in your family: 2 in 5

Percentage of people who will at some time marry or live
with an alcoholic:

- for women: 14%
- for men: 4%

Odds that a child will become an alcoholic in his or her lifetime: 1 in 18.

The average U.S. adult each year drinks:

- 35 gallons of beer
- 3 gallons of wine
- 2 gallons of spirits

The most common drug involved in hospital emergency room visits: alcohol.

Percentage of men who drink alcohol: 70%. Women: 50%.

French studies indicate that the consumption of between 1 and 5 glasses of wine daily lowers the risk of heart attack—even among those, like the French, who have a very rich diet.

RISK GEOGRAPHY

State with the largest number of dry counties: Kentucky.

Each year, more than ¾ of a million automobile crashes involve drinking drivers.

Percentage of drowning victims under the influence of alcohol: 10%.

Amid all the gloom and doom about the ill effects of alcohol, it is worth observing that the following seem to be beneficial effects of moderate drinking (defined, for a man, as less than 3 drinks per day and, for a woman, 2 drinks or less per day).

- relief of stress and anxiety
- lower risk of death from coronary disease
- increased estrogen levels in postmenopausal women
- decreased risk of strokes caused by artery blockage

Social drinkers have lower cholesterol levels, fewer heart attacks, and generally fewer head colds than teetotalers.

Moderate consumption of alcohol also appears to lower the risk of having both gallstones and coronary heart disease.

5

Beating the Odds on Disease

Few risk worries are as persistent as those touching on our health. The choices we make in our lives are often driven by such concerns. Most of us decide what to eat, whether to exercise, and what habits to adopt or avoid largely with a view to staying as healthy as we can. The fact that we are preoccupied with staying, or getting, healthy makes us prey to all manner of prophets pedaling cures and health regimens. Sometimes, these approaches are heavy on the snake oil and light on scientific validity. Other times, practices that began as quirky health fads become institutionalized in our way of life. (Breakfast cereals, for instance, were originally the preserve of the health faddists. Strenuous exercise was formerly associated with a group of crazies known as the physical culture movement.)

Our preoccupation with health is scarcely surprising. According to the American Medical Association, the average American lives about 28,000 days. He or she will be ill 4,400 days—about ⅙ of one's lifetime. The thought that there might be something that each of us can do to alter that ratio in our favor drives our fixation on living healthily. But that fixation is frustrated by the medical experts, who often seem unable to get their act together. Yesterday's recommended practice becomes today's pariah. Consider, for instance, the saga of health and exercise. For years, physicians have been telling us that moderate exercise is good for our health. Recent trials, including a vast study of some 17,000 Harvard alumni, now seem to suggest that moderate exercise is of little use and that nothing short of strenuous activity will significantly increase longevity. How long this consensus will endure is anybody's guess.

Many of the numbers that follow will show major differences between men's and women's health risks. It has been fashionable of late to charge medical researchers with having a bias for conducting studies on men and ignoring the health problems of women. The major investigation of sex bias in health-related research projects during the decade from 1983 to 1993 discovered that most studies (75%) focused on men and women alike. Among the studies devoted to a single sex, 12% involved only men while 13% involved only women. So, there appears to be little substance to the claim that men's health problems are getting the lion's share of the attention.

The interesting point is that even if it were true that more research dollars were devoted to men's medical problems than to those of women, this would not necessarily be unreasonable. Ponder one salient fact: Women are currently living about 7–8 years longer than men. There is nothing inevitable or even normal about a discrepancy so large. At the turn of this century, the difference in longevity between the sexes was about 2–3 years. Medicine and public health, so far this century, have done much more to extend the longevity of women than of men. Nowadays, on average, men get chronic and debilitating diseases much earlier than women do. Among men and women of the same age, a man is 50% more likely to have a heart attack before his next birthday than a woman is. Under such circumstances, there is a case to be made that men's medical problems are generally more in need of a solution than are women's. After all, we spend a great deal of money researching such diseases as AIDS and breast cancer, precisely on the grounds that they claim the lives of many hundreds of thousands of people well before their time.

SOME FAMILIAR KILLERS

You are at heightened risk for diabetes if:

- you are 45+
- you are black
- you have a family history of the disease

Fully one-third of whites 80+ have diabetes.

About 1 in every 300 Americans is a carrier of hepatitis B, which attacks the liver. Roughly a quarter of those will, at some stage in their lives, develop chronic hepatitis. A man is twice as likely to have it as a woman. It is especially common among people working in health care, drug users, and homosexuals. An infected pregnant mother runs a 70% risk of passing it on to her child.

You are more at risk for cirrhosis of the liver if you:

- drink
- are 40+
- are male

Roughly one-half of the homeless in the United States have latent tuberculosis; 7% have active tuberculosis.

Risk that you'll have a heart attack this year: 1 in 160. If you do, risk that you won't survive it: 1 in 3.

You are 50% more likely to have a heart attack on Monday than on any other day of the week.

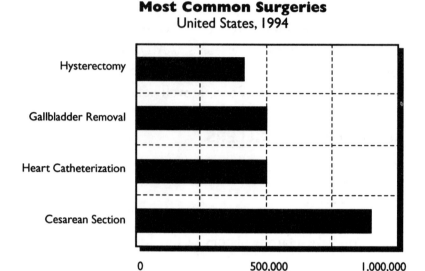

Most Common Surgeries
United States, 1994

You are at enhanced risk for heart attack if you:

- smoke
- have high serum cholesterol
- have a sedentary lifestyle
- are fat
- have high blood pressure

Some studies suggest that taller men have fewer heart attacks than shorter men do. Specifically, for each extra inch of height above the average (5 feet 10 inches), the heart attack risk shrinks by about 2%. No one knows the reason for this effect.

Contrary to popular impression, a high level of cholesterol is not a disease in itself. Rather, it is a *risk factor* for genuine diseases (for example, heart disease). While it is true that people with naturally low cholesterol levels tend to live longer than others, it is not established that Herculean efforts to lower your cholesterol level after the fact (through diet or drugs, for instance) do much good. Although your risk of heart disease *may* go down slightly if you successfully lower your cholesterol level, several studies suggest that your rate of mortality will probably *not* change significantly (in part because your risk of death from other causes rises).

Although high cholesterol is a risk factor for heart disease for those under 70, for older Americans there is no correlation between cholesterol levels and cardiovascular problems.

Odds that a black person has the sickle-cell trait: about 1 in 10.

You are at heightened risk for strokes if you:

- are older (45+)
- are black
- have high blood pressure
- have diabetes
- smoke

You are at heightened risk for hypertension if you:

- are black
- are obese
- have a family history of hypertension

By contrast, here are the annual risks that you will acquire several rare diseases that receive attention out of all proportion to their occurrence:

rabies	0.003%
Lyme disease	0.003%
tuberculosis	0.01%
hepatitis	0.01%
syphilis	0.01%
gonorrhea	0.2%.

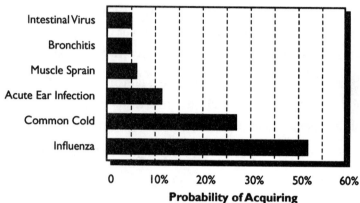

Risk of Common Diseases
Probability This Year

Probability of Acquiring

SOME NONFATAL NUISANCES

Women are twice as likely as men to suffer from irritable bowel syndrome (IBS).

About half of all visits to the doctor for gastrointestinal problems involve IBS.

Odds that you'll experience back pain sometime during the next 6 weeks: 50%.

You are at enhanced risk for anemia if you are:

- an infant
- a teenage girl
- a menstruating woman

As loathe as animal lovers are to admit it, pets can be a potent source of disease in the home. In fact, roughly 30% of all fatal human diseases are carried by other animals (chiefly mammals and insects). Both dogs and cats carry roundworm; some 95% of puppies born in the United States have it. Cats are carriers of toxoplasmosis, which can cause miscarriage in humans. Dogs and cats, as well as most farm-yard animals, can pass ringworm to humans. Domesticated birds like parrots and parakeets often have parrot fever, which causes serious symptoms in humans. Moreover, dogs often carry ticks, which in turn can be carriers of Lyme disease or Rocky Mountain spotted fever. Beyond this, humans can get rabies, cat scratch fever, strep throat, and *Salmonella* infections from their furry friends.

Worried about baldness? Don't attach too much importance to all those hairs in your brush because the average healthy adult sheds about 100 head hairs each day.

Odds that a man over 60 will be bald: 2 to 1.

Odds that a preteen girl has head lice: 1 in 15.

We tend to think of youngsters as the principal victims of accidental poisonings. The fact is that those over 65 are twice as likely to be hospitalized for poisoning as any other age group.

Most likely part of the body to receive plastic surgery: the nose.

Proportion of face-lifts performed on men: 1 in 11.

Odds that you presently have at least one medical device implanted in your body: 5%. Most such devices are made of silicone.

SOME MYSTERIES ABOUT BREAST IMPLANTS

Percentage of those with breast implants who are men: 2%

Percentage of those with breast implants who are white: 99%

One-in-every-three persons who has one implant has at least one other.

Artificial Inplants
United States, 1995

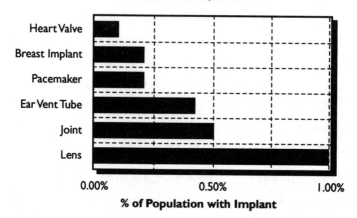

Number of cavities the average 15-year-old has in his or her teeth: 8.

You are more likely to develop *dental cavities* if you are:
- female
- young

You are at enhanced risk for gallstones if you:
- are female
- are older
- are fat
- have given birth to several children

Four million U.S. children contract chicken pox very year. About 9,000 are hospitalized because of it. Some 100 of those will die from complications.

Of those who develop measles, 98% are unvaccinated.

The latex allergy—which has only recently been studied scientifically—has become a serious problem in the medical profession. About 8% of operating room doctors and nurses and some 14% of dentists have developed an allergy to it. This means no rubber gloves or masks, no rubber hoses, no contact with adhesive tape, and so on.

Odds that an American boy will be circumcised: 2 in 3.

You are at greater risk for osteoporosis if you are:

- older (40+)
- female
- white

Recent research suggests that heavy-duty weight lifting twice a week can reduce the likelihood of a woman developing osteoporosis.

The most commonly cited complaints associated with sick building syndrome are headaches, dizziness, and disorientation.

Speaking of headaches, about 1% of the U.S. adult population develops headaches on any given day.

ALLERGIES IN THE WORKPLACE

Many jobs require workers to be around substances to which many people are allergic. Among the more common are these:

animal handlers	feathers, urine, dander
bakers	wheat protein
beauticians	henna
florists	pollen
health workers	latex
pharmaceutical workers	penicillin and similar drugs
postal workers	glue
sewage workers	sewer flies, mealworm
welders	stainless-steel fumes

About 1 in 5 women get migraine headaches.

Something to look forward to? If you survive to your late 70s, your odds of having Alzheimer's disease are 1 in 3. The risk intensifies with age. Specifically, those over 65 have a 10% chance of having Alzheimer's; those over 85 stand a 50% chance.

Odds that a random sample of medical waste is infectious: 1 in 8.

Worldwide, 5 million children die each year from diarrhea.

The World Health Organization estimates that at least 100 million tourists each year suffer from some type of diarrhea as a result of their travels. (Small wonder that vivid names like Hong Kong dog, Delhi belly, and Montezuma's revenge have become so commonplace.)

Among U.S. tourists who visit the tropics, the chance of getting of diarrhea is about 20–50%, depending on location.

About 15% of Mexican tourists in the United States develop diarrhea during their stay.

Risk that you are often constipated: 10%. If over 65: 20%.

Women are more likely to be constipated than men.

Most laxatives are strong enough to show up in a mother's milk in sufficiently strong doses to cause diarrhea in babies.

Risk that you will receive blood this year: 1 in 50.

Your risk of getting common respiratory infections is heightened if you:

- smoke or live around a smoker
- have a large family
- are under 10

SEEING THE DOCTOR

Number of prescriptions you will have filled this year: 6–7.

A woman is 15% more likely than a man to be ill. She will go to a doctor 50% more often and to the dentist 30% more often.

Proportion of Americans who are in the hospital on any given day: 1 in 300.

Odds that you will have an operation requiring a hospital stay this year: 1 in 12.

Percentage of physicians who are imposters: 2%.

> ### HISTORY IN A BOX
>
> The consensus among historians of medicine is that throughout most of the past, it was more dangerous to go to the hospital for treatment than to tough it out at home. The odds shifted in the other direction around the beginning of this century.

Odds that your doctor will be sued for malpractice this year: 2%. Annual premium your doctor pays for malpractice insurance: $15,000+.

Wonder why Medicare costs kept spiraling upward? Apart from malpractice issues and the explosive costs of high-tech medicine, a large part of the answer is that, on average, those over 65 see a doctor once a month. By contrast, those under 65 see a doctor 3–4 times per year. If a visit a month seems excessive, ponder the fact that the average older American has a 65% chance of being dizzy on any given day and a 60% chance of feeling pain on a random day.

Speaking of visiting the doctor, the average delay in a physician's waiting room is 21 minutes.

The scourge of the American Medical Association: 4% of the U.S. population has not been to a physician in the last 5 years.

RISK GEOGRAPHY

State with the fewest physicians per capita: Alaska.

Alaska also has the nation's highest charges for a hospital stay.

Odds you have not seen a doctor in the last 2 years: 1 in 10.

Odds that your doctor will report that your health is only fair or poor: 10%.

Wonder why your last hospital bill was so exorbitant? For every patient in a hospital bed, there are 6 hospital employees.

YOUR WORST NIGHTMARE

Polls show repeatedly that 9 out of 10 ordinary Americans believe that we are living through a cancer epidemic; fewer than one-third of cancer scientists agree. Two of three Americans believe that even tiny doses of carcinogens can produce cancer. Barely one-quarter of cancer specialists agree.

In fact, apart from lung cancer, no major forms of cancer are showing increased rates of incidence (when adjusted for the shifting age of the population).

A man is twice as likely to die of lung cancer as a woman.

Your overall risk of getting cancer is heightened if you:
- smoke
- are fat
- are over 50

You are at heightened risk for lung cancer if you:
- smoke
- are male
- are older
- are financially well-off

You are at heightened risk for stomach cancer if you are:

- male
- poor

You are at heightened risk for colorectal cancer if you:

- live in an urban area
- eat a high-fat diet
- have a family history of the disease

You are at heightened risk for pancreatic cancer if you are:

- male
- black

You are at heightened risk for prostate cancer if you are:

- older (45+)
- black

Each year, about 180,000 new cases of breast cancer occur among Americans. About one-quarter of those will prove fatal.

In the interpretation of mammograms designed to detect breast cancer, doctors often find evidence on the film that initially arouses their suspicions. In 80% of those cases, it is a false alarm (that is, a false-positive). Only about 1% of mammograms reveal something sufficiently suspicious to warrant a biopsy. Even then, about a third of the time, the biopsy reveals no evidence of cancer. The lesson should be clear: Where breast cancer is concerned, you should not assume the worst—until and unless there is solid biopsy evidence.

1 in every 100 whites with breast cancer is a man. 1 in every 50 blacks with breast cancer is a man.

Even at those ages when a woman is most at risk for breast cancer (that is, 45+), her chance of acquiring breast cancer in any given year is less than 1 in 250.

You are at heightened risk for breast cancer if you:

- are female
- are wealthy
- are Jewish
- are white or black (Asians have much lower rates)
- have had frequent chest X rays
- are unmarried
- had your first child after 30
- had menarche before age 12
- are fat and 50+
- are thin and under 50
- have a mother *and* sister with breast cancer

All of the following have been identified in at least one study as risk factors for breast cancer (a note of caution, however: few of these linkages have been robustly documented):

- smoking a few cigarettes during a lifetime
- weighing more than 8 pounds at birth
- exposure to magnetic fields
- having an abortion
- having unusually long or short menstrual cycles
- using olive oil
- having a first child later than normal
- living near a toxic waste dump

Odds that a man will someday have fatal cancer of the penis: 1 in 28,000.

You are at heightened risk for cancer of the penis if you :

- have had 30 or more lifetime sexual partners
- have not been circumcised
- smoke cigarettes

Women who have their first child after the age of 33 are 40% less likely to develop ovarian cancer than those women who have their first child before they are 20.

Consumption of dietary vitamin A appears to lower the risk of lung cancer; a shortage of beta-carotene increases the probability of lung cancer.

Among people under 30, those who use tanning lamps are 3 times more likely to develop melanoma than average.

Several forms of cancer are infectious (for example, cancer of the spine), especially through sexual contact.

Estrogen lowers the risk of heart disease for postmenopausal women; however, estrogen probably raises the risk of breast cancer by 10% or more.

Women over 50 who take estrogen-replacement therapy are about 50% less likely to develop colon cancer than those who do not.

People living in rich countries are at greater risk for cancer of the breast, colon, and uterus than those living in poor countries. By contrast, stomach cancer is more prevalent in poor countries.

STATES OF MIND

Odds you will have some sort of serious mental disorder in your lifetime: 1 in 2.

Chances you will be admitted to a mental hospital this year: 0.3%.

Women cry about 4 times more often than men.

Speaking of mental disease, it remains a source of enormous embarrassment to the psychiatric profession that psychiatrists have a hard time agreeing among themselves about how to diagnose it. For instance, in one well-known study of 100 mental patients who saw two different psychiatrists, *only 21 patients received the same diagnosis*. Concerning another 25 patients, the psychiatrists could not agree whether they were dealing with a psychosis or not.

In almost every society, including the United States, women are more likely than men to have a major bout of depression. Canadian women are twice as likely as U.S. women to have this problem. French and German women are 3–4 times more likely to have it than their U.S. counterparts. The constant, amid all these variations, is that the men in each of these societies exhibit depression only about half as often as the women.

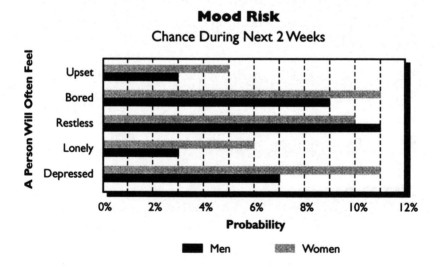

Mood Risk
Chance During Next 2 Weeks

Women are also likely to remain depressed longer than men and to have their first episode of depression at a younger age than men.

WHEN THE CURE IS WORSE THAN THE DISEASE

We go to the doctor because we expect a cure for whatever ails us, but everybody knows that treatment often introduces risks of its own. There is now an entire medical specialty (called iatrogenics) devoted to treating the nasty side effects of the use of medication. That's not surprising when you consider that about one-quarter of the patients given drugs during hospital stays develop some sort of adverse reaction to their medication.

About 1 in 200 hospital patients develops a *fatal* reaction to their medication. In most of these cases, the patients were suffering from severe terminal illnesses and the medicines were utilized as a last resort or to relieve intensive pain and suffering. In terms of *preventable* deaths, the rate of medication-caused death among hospital patients is about 1 in 10,000.

About 1 in every 1,000 hospital patients who receives heavy doses of aspirin becomes deaf.

It is not just in-patient hospital care that produces the problem: Approximately 1 in every 2,000 infants receiving pertussis vaccine against whooping cough will have a very negative reaction (typically involving shock and convulsions).

An unvaccinated child who develops whooping cough runs a 1 in 50 chance of going into shock or convulsions.

A child who goes through the usual battery of 5 DPT vaccinations runs a 1 in 90 chance of some form of alarming reaction.

The standard vaccines given for diphtheria, tetanus, measles, and hepatitis B are all capable of causing anaphylaxis—a sudden, rare, and potentially life-threatening reaction.

Vaccines for diphtheria and polio can also trigger Guillain-Barré syndrome (a serious nerve disease).

Middle-aged and elderly patients are often told by their doctors to have an angiogram, which uses a catheter to explore the coronary arteries. Approximately 2–3 in every 1,000 persons who undergo this procedure die as a result of the test, from either a stroke or heart attack induced by the procedure.

About 5–6% of women on the pill develop serious depression.

A MEDICAL GRAB BAG

Roughly 40% of the U.S. adult population dye their hair frequently. Some studies suggest that, especially among those who use dark hair dyes, there is a slight increase in the risk for leukemia and lymphoma.

Toxic shock syndrome (TSS), a potentially fatal condition, has long been associated with the use of tampons. During the last 15 years, the incidence of TSS related to menstruation has shrunk from more than 1,000 cases per year to about 50 cases.

Chances that an episode of TSS will be fatal: 5%.

The only organ *unlikely* to succeed after a transplant is the lung.

The virus *Ebola*, most recently involved in an epidemic in Zaire, kills more than 90% of its victims, usually within 1 week of the appearance of the first symptoms. (There have been four outbreaks in the last two decades.) The rapidity with which *Ebola* claims its victims explains why the outbreaks are generally locally confined. The carriers scarcely live long enough to pass it along outside of their immediate circle.

Chances that a heat stroke incident will be fatal: 15%.

During a severe heat wave, death rates among the elderly in the affected locality can temporarily increase by 50%. Women are more likely to be affected than men.

Your odds of dying this year from exposure to cold: 1 in 300,000.

The poets were right: The young are more likely to die in summer than in winter. The old are more likely to die in winter than summer.

If you store in your closet or wear freshly dry-cleaned clothes, your blood will have higher than normal levels of the carcinogen tetrachloroethane.

According to a pilot study done by the Food and Drug Administration, a woman's risk of having a negative reaction to her next use of cosmetics: 1 in 1,500.

6

The House from Hell— Probably Yours

Everyone knows the adage about how accidents happen in the "safety" of our own homes. For a change, this is a risk cliché that has some truth to it. If you doubt it, ponder the fact that the chances that you will be seriously injured at home in some fashion this year are 23%. (An injury counts as serious for these purposes if it requires immediate, emergency medical treatment.) The average injury in the home costs about $300 in medical treatment and involves an additional $900 in lost wages or salary. That figure translates into some 60 million Americans being injured each year around the house at a cost of some $75 billion.

What you may *not* know is just how many risk points there are lurking around the house. They say that familiarity breeds contempt. It certainly seems right that most of us are oblivious to the domestic risks we have been living with all our lives. Here is a partial guided tour to some of them. By way of sensitizing yourself to them anew (or, in some cases, probably for the first time), imagine that you grew up in the Australian outback or some African jungle, entirely devoid of modern conveniences, and are being shown around a twentieth-century house for the first time. Your guide is a risk nut keen to warn you of the dangers lurking about. Alternatively, approach your own house as a future archaeologist, bent on discovering its risks, might.

THE KITCHEN

Altogether, well over 1 million Americans each year are seriously injured in their kitchens. The chief culprit—causing 460,000 of those injuries—is, as you might expect, cutlery. Each of us runs about a 0.2% risk annually of serious injury from kitchen knives.

Next in the queue is drinking glasses. Teenagers are the chief victims here, with 1 in every 1,000 getting seriously cut by a glass each year.

Tableware is a close runner-up, again with teenagers having the greatest problem managing their plates, knives, and forks.

The last noteworthy kitchen risk is the oven/range, responsible for about 50,000 injuries per year. Those most at risk from ovens are toddlers, coming in at a level of 0.1%.

THE LIVING ROOM

Handily beating the kitchen as a risk source is your average living/family room. Chairs alone injure more than 400,000 of us each year, especially toddlers (who are at a 0.7% risk of serious harm) and seniors (0.3% risk).

Tables produce almost as many injuries and are even riskier for toddlers than are chairs.

Desks and cabinets likewise claim their toll, about a quarter million, especially among toddlers (0.3%).

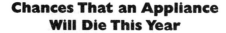

Chances That an Appliance Will Die This Year

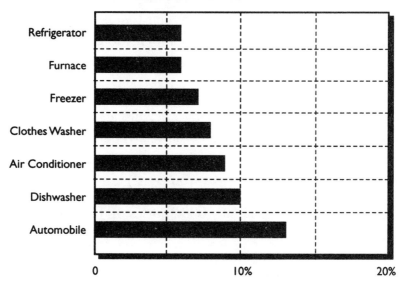

Rugs and carpets send about 130,000 people to the hospital each year.

Stereo systems and televisions produce about 100,000 injuries. By the way, the chances that your television set will catch fire sometime this year is about 1 in 7,500.

THE BATH

True to their reputation, tubs and showers are the chief culprits here, producing upward of 150,000 serious injuries per year (including 1 in every 500 infants). Still worse, 70 children die in the tub. Curiously, less than a third of those deaths are caused by drowning. Most are caused by hot water scalds (that is, water above 125 degrees Fahrenheit). Sadly, studies show that fewer than 3% of the parents of young children know the temperature of their hot water heater.

A close second to tubs in the injury sweepstakes are toilets (45,000 injuries). It would be fascinating to know how so many people injure themselves on their toilets, but unfortunately the feds do not collect such information. Three infants every year die of drowning in a toilet; a similar number drown in diaper pails.

The bathroom poses a number of other threats that are less visible. More than 40,000 men each year require emergency treatment for shaving injuries. (A man is twice as likely to injure himself with a razor as a woman is.)

Hair dryers cause another 15,000 injuries. In fact, prior to the mandating of safety plugs for dryers in 1991, about 20 Americans electrocuted themselves each year when their dryers fell into tubs and basins.

Another less-than-safe gadget in the bathroom is the hair curling iron. About 2,000 infants each year receive serious burns from them, whereas 500 teenagers manage to stick a hot curling iron into their eye.

And we shouldn't forget the medicine cabinet, as 1 in every 250 infants is poisoned (usually nonfatally) by some medication intended for an adult. You might have thought that the development of childproof caps for drugs would eliminate this problem. Official government figures make it clear that the mandating of such caps saves less than 1 child per 1 million each year.

THE BEDROOM

Place of peace and tranquility? Anything but! Some 400,000 of us each year are seriously injured by our beds. Everything from falling out of them, to falling down with them, to injuring a body part on the bedstead. Still worse, some people, especially infants, suffocate in them. (An infant is far more likely to suffocate in the parents' bed than in his or her own.)

The clothing in the closets also takes its toll: 150,000 Americans are seriously injured by their clothing every year.

And, improbably, about 100,000 of us get rushed to emergency rooms because our shoes or shoe laces have not performed as designed.

Jewelry causes another 50,000 injuries, mostly to the under 5s.

As for that money some of us keep under the mattress, hospital admission records indicate that about 28,000 people each year require treatment at a trauma center caused by handling or swallowing cash.

Most houses have draperies in the bedroom. Not too good an idea; 20 people every year are accidentally strangled to death on drapery cords.

Perhaps you keep a pair of scissors somewhere in the bedroom. Over a decade, 1 in every 100 adults lives to regret that decision since they end up in a hospital emergency room suffering from a scissors stab.

Somehow, 6,000 adults every year manage to injure themselves on the bedclothes!

THE KIDS' ROOM

To no one's surprise, toys are the chief culprit, producing about 150,000 injuries each year. Rather more surprising is the fact that 1 in every 4 injuries caused by a toy is to an adult.

Speaking of toys, you should be aware that toys available in the United States are tough! Before a toy product can be labeled as suitable for children *under* 18 months of age, the manufacturer must show that it will survive intact and undamaged after 10 successive drops from about 5 feet high onto a hard surface. Traditional toys like crayons—which could not possibly survive such a standard—were grand-fathered in when the law was passed. Future inventions of the same type will not be available to this age group.

Cribs and playpens are much safer than adult beds, even to young children, producing only about 15,000 injuries per year. The curious twist again is that about 20% of all the injuries caused by cribs are to adults.

THE GARAGE AND BASEMENT

These rooms turn out to be a virtual cesspool of nasty risks. Ladders and stools injure about 200,000 every year, especially seniors.

Nails and screws produce about 250,000 serious injuries.

Saws, both manual and power, account for another 100,000 injuries, roughly two-thirds of them to men.

Other manual tools cause about 160,000 visits to emergency rooms.

Odds that you will crush a finger with a hammer this year: 1 in 3,000.

Lawnmowers produce roughly 80,000 injuries and 75 deaths annually, mostly to men. A single gas-powered lawn mower can generate as much air pollution (especially carbon monoxide and benzene) in 1 hour of operation as a new car generates in driving 5,000 miles.

About 10 children die each year being crushed by an automatic garage door. Buckets and pails injure about 12,000 people every year. Some 50 toddlers die each year by drowning in a 5-gallon bucket.

ANYWHERE

The single biggest risk in a household is the stairway. Roughly 2 million Americans take a serious fall on them each year. Toddlers and seniors run a 1.5% chance of being injured on stairs. Although men are at home fewer hours each week than women, they are about 50% more likely to injure themselves on stairs than women are.

Half a million of us injure ourselves on doors, especially glass doors. Young adults are particularly at risk on this one.

Household wiring electrocutes about 300 people annually.

Windows cause injuries to about 60,000. Seventy Americans die every year falling out of them.

Odds that you will be seriously injured on your Christmas decorations this year: 1 in 65,000.

17,000 people injure themselves on their telephones. A more serious worry, that cellular phones may be linked to cancer, appears not to be borne out, as reported in a lengthy German study on the subject. On the other hand, cellular phones are not risk-free—at least not when they are used in an automobile. A 1993 study showed that drivers with cellular phones are 34% more likely to have an accident than those without.

About 300 persons every year die in their homes (often trailers) from the fumes of natural gas and propane.

Many Americans have been persuaded to buy carbon monoxide monitors for their homes to protect themselves from this silent killer, which is odorless and colorless. Few of them probably realize that they are 300% more likely to be accidentally poisoned by carbon monoxide in their cars than in their homes.

> ### HOW GAS GOT ITS SMELL
>
> As it comes from the ground, natural gas is odorless. What we think of as the smell of natural gas is an odorant added to allow its detection. The odorant began to be added after a gas explosion in a Texas school in 1937 claimed almost 300 victims.

THE BACKYARD

The family swimming pool causes about 100,000 serious injuries annually. Some 300 children die every year in home swimming and wading pools. According to the Consumer Product Safety Commission, there are cases in which children sat on the drain holes of in-ground wading pools and had their intestines sucked from their bodies.

> ### RISK ENHANCERS
>
> You have a heightened risk of drowning if you are:
>
> • under 10
> • over 75

Hot tubs produce about 5,000 injuries. Every year, a handful of Americans, usually female, die of drowning because their hair gets drawn into the suction drain of a hot tub.

Backyard fences cause 125,000 serious injuries.

Every year, 45,000 children are injured on *home* playground equipment. Another 200,000 are injured on playground equipment away from the home. The principal culprit, accounting for 68% of the injuries, is the swing set.

OTHER RISKS AROUND THE HOUSE

If you live in a house with older plumbing, you are likely to have unsafe levels of lead in your tap water. If you can't afford to replace the plumbing, experts recommend using only cold water for drinking and cooking, because lead is much less soluble in cold water than in hot.

According to the Environmental Protection Agency, 12% of U.S. homes have unacceptably high radon levels. Radon is a known cause of cancer. (It should be added that the United States sets more stringent standards for radon exposure than most other industrialized countries.)

HOUSEHOLD POLLUTANTS

Many of the dangers around the house do not produce immediate injury but are nonetheless risky. Household pollution is one example. Common sources of indoor air pollution are:

carbon monoxide	gas and kerosene heaters, furnaces and fireplaces, tobacco smoke
formaldehyde	plywood and particle board, textiles, foam insulation
lead	soldering, burning, or sanding of lead paint; plumbing
mercury	certain latex paints

Cosmetics and Allergies

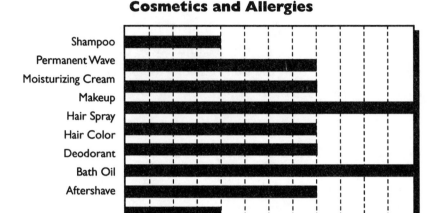

	Low	Medium	High
Shampoo			
Permanent Wave			
Moisturizing Cream			
Makeup			
Hair Spray			
Hair Color			
Deodorant			
Bath Oil			
Aftershave			

If you use mothballs or toilet deodorants, your breath will exhibit higher than normal levels of the carcinogen paradichlorobenzene.

And you thought the bottled water got you off the hook: By taking a shower a day in chlorinated water, you inhale or absorb through the skin as much chloroform as drinking 2 quarts of tap water daily.

Odds that your house is more than half a century old: 1 in 3. Why is this a risk? Well, houses more than 50 years old are more likely to have electrical fires, unsafe levels of lead in the drinking water, dangerous forms of insulation (such as asbestos), and radon in the basement than newer houses.

Risk that your home will have a serious fire this year: 1 in 160.

A *functioning* smoke detector will cut your risk of dying in a fire by one-half.

RISK ENHANCERS

Your risk of dying from fire or burns this year is heightened if you are 75+.

Proportion of installed smoke detectors that would not detect a fire (for example, because of dead batteries): 1 in 3.

Likelihood that you never check the batteries in your smoke detector: 65%.

Up-scale residences are now being built with automatic sprinkler systems installed. Such systems do lower your risk of dying in a fire at home, but they are not foolproof. Apart from occasionally causing water damage by going off when there is no fire, roughly 1 in every 100 systems fails to operate when it should. Another 5% of them will move into action but will fail to control the fire.

Some people are worried about the health effects of exposure to strong magnetic fields. They probably shouldn't be because the earth's own magnetic field is much stronger than those usually encountered from high-voltage lines or electrical appliances.

If, nonetheless, you are inclined to worry about this risk, you might want to ponder the fact that people who sleep under electric blankets are exposed to

THE KLUTZ FACTOR

Some of the ways we injure ourselves around the home boggle my limited imagination. Here are a few, with the annual numbers attached. See if you can figure them out.

musical instruments	8,000
fabrics	8,000
books and magazines	7,000
blankets	6,000
faucets	5,700
baby bottles	5,000
pillows	4,000
computers	4,000
room deodorizers	3,300
crayons	3,000
toilet bowl products	2,200
ironing boards	2,000
flashlights	2,000
balloons	2,000

magnetic fields 10–100 times stronger than those found elsewhere in the home. Existing studies of users of electric blankets show no evidence of increased risk of cancer.

A recurrent theme of this book is that we are constantly facing risk trade-offs. Doing something to minimize one risk often puts us at greater risk for a different threat. Here is another example. Studies have shown that the relative humidity in the home can have a dramatic effect on the number of allergies and respiratory infections that both children and adults suffer. For instance, children whose home and schools were humidified during the winter months missed school because of respiratory problems only 20% less than as those whose homes and schools were not humidified. So far, this looks like a good case for installing a humidifier in your home, right? Well, as usual, there is a snag—several in fact. One is this: If you let the humidity get too high (say, above 60%), this will encourage the growth of both mold and dust mites—to which many of us are allergic. Another is that unless you are assiduous about cleaning out the humidifier, the system itself can be a potent culture for bacteria and certain viruses.

7

The Maiming Fields, or No Pain No Gain

L et's begin this chapter with a quicky quiz. Which of these activities is the leading cause of serious injuries to those between ages 15 and 50?

a. accidents at home
b. accidents on the job
c. motor vehicle accidents
d. none of the above

The right answer is d, because the *principal* cause of injuries requiring emergency medical treatment is sports.

If this strikes you as odd, it probably should; for it is not an easy piece of information to come by. The media haven't discovered it yet; the government has no high-profile watchdog agency charged with monitoring the problem. But it is no less real for its extraordinarily low profile. Each year, more than 4 million Americans are injured playing some sport or other (and this figure underreports the problem because it excludes all accidents related to sport biking). Given how dangerous sports are, you might think that public health officials would take steps to discourage them. Far from it—the feds go out of their way to encourage everyone, especially youth, to participate in organized sports. After all, we are told, it builds character, instills a sense of teamwork, and provides good exercise. So it may; but it likewise costs money, causes pain, and takes lives.

If we narrow our focus to those groups most likely to participate in sports—namely, men and boys from 5 to 24— the risks of sports take on even more sinister proportions. For instance, among boys 5–14, football alone produces more injuries than all motor vehicle accidents in which boys of this age are involved in as passengers. Between them, baseball and football produce twice as many injuries to boys of this age as motor vehicles do.

Things must be different, you might imagine, as these boys become young men and start driving cars themselves. After all, men in the 15–24 age group have notoriously bad driving records. Although vehicle injuries do indeed skyrocket for men in this cohort, sports still account for twice as many serious injuries. In fact, three sports alone—football, baseball, and basketball—injure more young men than cars do.

Because many men of this age are not participants in sports—while almost all drive or ride in motor vehicles—the comparison on a participant basis suggests that it is 500–600% more dangerous to participate in sports than to use a car.

In neither the case of cars nor sports are we dealing with trivial injuries, because these numbers come from patients injured sufficiently seriously to require emergency medical treatment. But that still leaves open the question of just *how* serious.

Besides, you might say, the most important issue in comparing such leisure-time activities is not so much the injuries involved as it is the people killed. There, of course, the automobile is a greater threat. But we shouldn't let sports off too lightly here either. Every year, about 5,000 Americans—

mostly males in the 5–24 age group—end up dead because they went swimming or diving or boating or jogging once too often. This number marks a greater loss of life than is caused by all the house fires, burns, and explosions in the nation.

SPORTS

In general, a woman runs about one-quarter the risk of a man of sustaining a serious sports injury.

In almost all sports, men are more likely to be injured than women. The three exceptions are bowling, gymnastics, and volleyball.

You are more likely to injure yourself on a bicycle than on a skateboard.

Each year about half a dozen boxers, amateur and pro, are killed in the ring.

Risk that a professional hockey player will lose at least one tooth to the sport in his career: 68%.

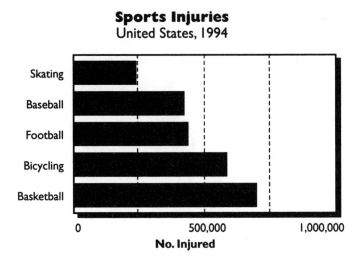

Sports Injuries
United States, 1994

Odds that a high-school football player will make it to the pros: 1 in 1,200. Odds that he will make an NCAA team: 1 in 20.

Odds that a college athlete will not graduate: 1 in 2. Odds in the PAC10 Conference: 9 in 10.

Risk of a fatal accident this year if you are a rock climber: 1 in 20,000.

The numbers in the table on page 131 give us a good idea of how many accidents occur in various leisure-time activities, but they tell us nothing about the *relative risks* of different activities, as different numbers of people participate in different activities. For instance, the fact that 34,000 people are injured dancing whereas only 1,000 are injured scuba diving obviously does not mean that the latter activity is safer than the former. Here are *relative* risks for some leisure activities:

table tennis	1 injury per 9,500 participants
billiards	1 per 5,000
badminton	1 per 3,500
skateboarding	1 per 1,300
bowling	1 per 1,200
archery	1 per 900
golf, fishing	1 per 600
water skiing, surfboarding, tennis	1 per 500
exercising with equipment	1 per 400
snowmobiling	1 per 300
roller skating, ice skating, racket ball, volleyball	1 per 200
horseback riding	1 per 100
bicycle riding	1 per 80
baseball	1 per 70
basketball	1 per 40
football, ice hockey	1 per 30

SOME LEISURE-TIME INJURY FIGURES

soccer	121,000	snowmobiles	17,000
track and field	114,000	water skiing	16,000
swing sets	94,000	go-carts	15,000
hockey	82,000	fireworks	13,000
monkey bars	80,000	squash	12,000
fishing	78,000	diving boards	11,000
toys	78,000	camping	11,000
swimming pools	74,000	seesaws	10,000
riding	71,000	tricycles	10,000
weight lifting	60,000	kids' wagons	9,000
all-terrain vehicles	59,000	rugby	9,000
trampolines	53,000	musical instruments	8,000
slides	52,000	boxing	8,000
sleds	50,000	Jet Skis	8,000
golf	47,000	Christmas trees	7,000
swimming	45,000	beach chairs	7,000
gymnastics	39,000	books	7,000
mountain bikes	36,000	treehouses	6,000
dancing	34,000	hot tubs	5,000
martial arts	30,000	billiards	5,000
aquariums	28,000	archery	4,000
tennis	28,000	toy guns	3,000
skateboards	25,000	horseshoes	3,000
air rifles	23,000	marbles	2,000
bowling	21,000	scuba diving	1,000

A football player is more likely to be injured in practice than during a game. He is also much likelier to be injured early in the season than late.

Part of the body most frequently injured in football games: knee (20%).

Risk that a high-school football player this season will receive a disabling injury (which lasts a week or more): 35%

Baseball is just about as dangerous as football. Every year, 3–4 boys, ages 5–14, die from baseball injuries. Some 160,000 in that age group are seriously injured, and about half of those injuries are severe.

The most common age for baseball injuries is 12. Roughly half result from being hit by the ball; about 10% involve hits by the bat. The most common site for baseball injuries is the face.

About 1 in 10 student and professional athletes—who have no prior record of asthma— develop what is called exercise-induced asthma. Accordingly, after strenuous exercise, even many Olympic-class athletes require asthma drugs to restore normal breathing. This syndrome is especially common among runners and basketball players; it is less likely among swimmers, skiers, and gymnasts. Incidentally, the 67 asthmatics on the 1984 U.S. Summer Olympics team won 41 medals in the Los Angeles games.

Skateboards cause about 28,000 injuries annually, and ⅓ of all skateboard accidents happen to riders with less than 1 week of experience.

EXERCISE

Several million Americans regularly work out on exercise equipment. Of those, about 91,000 are injured each year. The annual risk of serious injury to frequent users is about 1 in 400.

A study by the RAND Corporation suggests that a sedentary person can add 21 minutes to his or her life span for each mile walked. Before you rush out to the track, you might ask yourself how long it takes you to walk that mile (including, if this is your usual routine, suiting up, driving to the site where the walk begins, and cleaning up afterward). It is quite likely that, all things considered, you will spend far more time on the effort than the 21 minutes of longer life that you gain. What it boils down to is that if you enjoy walking anyway, it is a useful way to extend your life. If you don't enjoy it, the gain is marginal or nonexistent.

> ### RISK GEOGRAPHY
>
> State with the highest percentage of couch potatoes: Mississippi (43%).
>
> State with the lowest percentage of CPs: Montana (17%).

Interestingly, although those who engage in vigorous off-the-job exercise cut their risks of carpal tunnel syndrome (CST) drastically, available data suggest that couch potatoes, who never exercise, are less likely to develop CST than are those who engage in light exercise programs.

If every able-bodied American would jog an hour a day, roughly 500 people would die each day from the exertion. (That's almost 200,000 deaths per year.) It's true, of course, that the survivors would live longer and be much fitter than the average American of today, but that is small comfort to those millions who would drop along the way.

Well, you might say, we can identify those most at risk from vigorous exercise by giving them a stress test before they start jogging. Not a great idea either: If every U.S. adult took the standard treadmill stress test, some 15,000–20,000 of them would suffer a fatal coronary event *during* the stress test itself.

8

Love, Marriage, and the Consequences

The Weaker Sex? This is a chapter principally about the fallout from the battle of the sexes. In these politically correct times, it is not in fashion to stick up for the male of the species. On the contrary, we often hear that men are more violent, more prone to crime, and less compassionate and caring than women. While all that may well be true, some recent proposals strike this (too defensive?) male as going a bit too far. For instance, in a recent book, *Men Are Not Cost-Effective* (New York: HarperPerennial, 1995), J. Stephenson proposed a special tax to be levied on all males. Her rationale is that disproportionate numbers of men in our society commit crimes and, to boot, end up in prisons, a serious net drain on our economic resources.

In the spirit of Ms. Stephenson's quest, I am minded to suggest quite the opposite, namely, a substantial tax *break* for the less than fair sex. My thinking is that since men are chronically put at greater risk of life and limb than women, they are entitled to a kind of hazardous duty pay for the gender roles they have inherited. Consider some of the relevant data.

Everyone knows that men are at risk of dying earlier than women. Although both sexes have been living longer since the turn of this century, the gap between average life expectancies

135

of the sexes has been widening dramatically. In 1900, a woman was likely to outlive a man by about 3 years. That spread is now closer to 7 years. How much is 7 extra years of life worth? Conservatively, say, $250,000.

Ms. Stephenson correctly observes that men are far more likely to be criminals than women. What she does not emphasize is that men also run a far greater risk (300%) of being the *victims* of violent crime, including homicide. Well, you say, it only stands to reason that if men are the criminals, they are likely to be shooting one another.

It is true that men shoot far more men than women. But, in one of those little noted ironies of modern crime, it turns out that women who commit murder are 5 times more likely to choose a male victim than a female one. The sad fact is that men and women alike disproportionately kill men. In this age of not blaming the victim, *who* should we be taxing here? (Incidentally, speaking of victims and tax dollars, the United States spends 20 times as much money counseling every female victim of violent crime as it spends on her male counterpart.)

Then there is the matter of accidents. There is virtually no major accident category where men are not at greater risk than women. Men are 3 times as likely to suffocate to death, 4 times more likely to be struck by lightning, 6 times more likely to die in a plane crash, 10 times more likely to fall off a ladder, 30 times more likely to be killed by police gunfire, and 60 times more likely to die in war.

Surely, you say, it's only natural that men will have higher rates of accidental death, because they tend to gravitate to the more dangerous professions where, perhaps, they are better compensated. But accident death rates for men are double those for women, including while working around the house or during their leisure time. Risk-related salary increments on the job, even where they exist, do not begin to touch these other dimensions of the accident-prone male's lifestyle.

Turn to figures about fatal diseases and the story repeats itself. A man between 50 and 70 is twice as likely to die of heart disease as a woman. He is twice as likely to succumb to tuberculosis and lung cancer. Even in infancy, the male risk profile looms large. A newborn boy is 25% more likely to die before his first birthday than his twin sister. Boys are twice as likely to die of sudden infant death syndrome as girls, and on it goes. Men, ages 15–24, are 600% more likely to commit suicide than women of those ages.

The bottom line comes to this: There is *never* an age, from birth through dotage, when the male death rate is not substantially higher than the female one.

Under the circumstances, let us scrap Ms. Stephenson's idea of a special male tax and institute instead a scheme of life-long hazardous duty pay for the males among us. If you don't like thinking of it as hazardous duty, the data invite another interpretation. Think of us males as suffering from a certain disability, a kind of klutziness gene that makes us much more accident-prone than women. Where the risks of ordinary life are concerned, the male is not differently abled—he is disabled, pure and simple. Under the new Americans with Disabilities Act, we might just qualify for some sort of special treatment

TYING AND UNTYING THE KNOT

Barely half of all weddings are first marriages.

The second time around: Contrary to popular belief, second marriages are not more likely to end in divorce than first marriages.

Husbands tend to be about 5 years older than their wives, but, for men who marry at 55+, the age gap widens to about 12 years.

Whenever there is talk about the imminent collapse of the American family, there is usually hand-wringing about the escalating divorce rate. This is partly a myth. Divorce rates were much higher in the late 1940s and early 1950s than they have been in the last 40 years.

The age group most at risk for divorce (for men and women): 25–29.

A German marriage is only half as likely to end in divorce as a U.S. one.

The highest divorce rate in the United States is found, of course, in Nevada. But because many of those are "quickie" divorces of persons living out of state, we should treat Nevada as a special case. Among the other 49 states, Oklahoma has the highest divorce rate; Massachusetts, at half Oklahoma's level, has the lowest.

The majority of both divorced men and divorced women will remarry, generally within 3 years of their divorce. Men are more likely to remarry than women.

Who's kidding whom? About half of all marriages end in divorce. Even so, some 3 out of 4 married couples, when asked about the state of their marriage, estimate that there is a "very low" chance their marriage will ever end in divorce.

Percentage of all married men who will eventually commit adultery: 50%. Of married women: 40%.

Lest you thought that adultery was a sign of the impending collapse of a marriage, you should bear in mind that 1 in 4 women who claim to be "happily married" have had extra-marital affairs.

If you're the average American married woman, the odds are about 1 in 3 that your husband has already cheated on you. Chances are greater than 1 in 10 that he has cheated within the past year.

For the average married man, there's a 1 in 4 chance that your wife has already committed adultery. Chances are about 1 in 14 that it was within the last year.

Chances that if you strongly suspect your spouse of having an affair, you are right: about 90%.

Although men still generally carry the burden of proposing marriage, it turns out that women are twice as likely as men to propose an end to a marriage and twice as likely to file for divorce.

Women may be proposing divorce but they are *not* profiting from it. A woman's economic situation a year after obtaining a divorce is likely to be 70% worse than before the divorce.

A man's situation is apt to be about 40% better than before a divorce.

Life span of the usual marriage in the United States: 8–9 years.

The average U.S. wedding costs about one-half the annual salary of an American worker. The average divorce settlement costs about 3 years' salary.

Proportion of women ages 15–44 who have lived with a boyfriend to whom they were not married: 1 in 3.

RISK FACTORS

You are at heightened risk for divorce if you are:

- poor
- less well-educated
- married very young
- have an interracial marriage
- conceived a child before marriage
- black
- Protestant

Odds that you'll eventually marry the person you're now living with: 50–50. For whites: about 55%; For blacks: about 42%.

Proportion of your life that you will spend unmarried: more than ½. This figure applies to men and women alike.

Only half of the divorced or separated women who are entitled to child support will receive the full amount.

Three-quarters of older husbands say that they *always* like their wives; only one-half of older wives say the same of their husbands.

The same difference shows up in responses to the question (to married couples): Would you marry the same person if you had it to do over again? A large majority of married men say yes: 80%; a bare majority of women do, 51%.

58% of men who divorce or separate say that they are happier afterward; 85% of women claim to be happier.

Odds that an unmarried 18-year-old will *never* marry: 5%.

A white woman is 3 times more likely to marry a black man than a white man is likely to marry a black woman.

Odds that a divorce involves children under 18: 3 in 5.

Odds that the custody of a child of a divorce will be awarded to the mother: 9 in 10.

A marriage that has produced only a son is less likely to end in divorce than a marriage that has produced only a daughter.

Like your parents? Sons are much more likely than daughters to rate their parents only fair or poor.

Despite this, men report far fewer problems with their in-laws than women do.

One of the best-kept secrets of modern family life: *Most* parents claim to be happier before they have children than after. Happiness returns to higher levels after children leave the nest.

PERPETUATING THE SPECIES

Percentage of babies born at home: 2.5%.

Percentage of babies born by a cesarean section: 25%.

Your risk of having a cesarean is heightened if you are over 35.

Chances that a baby will be seriously premature: 14%.

> **RISK GEOGRAPHY**
>
> A teenager aged 15–19 is most likely to be pregnant in Nevada (1 in 7). She is least likely to be pregnant in South Dakota (1 in 14).

Chances that a baby will weigh less than 2,500 grams (5.5 pounds.): 7%.

Chances that a couple who wishes to have children is involuntarily infertile: 15%.

Odds that this condition can be successfully treated: 85%.

If a couple is infertile, the odds that the infertility occurs in the woman: 2 in 3.

One of the principal predictors for infertility in a woman is a prior history of sexually transmitted diseases, especially ones that were not treated at an early stage.

Recent strides in DNA testing have enabled researchers to identify twins who share the same mother but have

> **RISK GEOGRAPHY**
>
> City with the highest infant death rate: Washington, D.C.

different fathers. Experts think that such births can occur when a woman ovulates twice during a single menstrual cycle and has sex with more than one man during that cycle.

Odds that a couple who wants to adopt a child will fail: 2 to 1.

About 1 in 4 first-time brides are pregnant or already mothers at the time of their wedding.

More than half of black brides are thus encumbered.

About one-quarter of all births are to unwed mothers.

Half of all black children born since 1986 have been illegitimate. About 15% of white children born in that period have been illegitimate.

A pregnant woman in New York State is 8 times more likely to have an abortion than a pregnant woman in Wyoming.

RISK GEOGRAPHY

A pregnant woman in California is 400% more likely to have an abortion than one in Utah.

In Mississippi, more than 1 in every 4 births is illegitimate. In Utah, fewer than 1 in 15 births is.

Most likely age group for a first abortion: 13–21.

Your risk of having twins is heightened if

- there is a history of multiple births in your family
- the mother is 30+

If both a child's parents are right-handed, the child's probability of being right-handed is 91%. If both parents are left-handed, the likelihood of a

---

TWIN RISKS

Odds that your next pregnancy will produce

- ordinary twins: about 1 in 90
- conjoined twins: 1 in 100,000

right-handed offspring is 63%. With mixed parents, the child has a 78% chance of being right-handed.

Most boy babies (2 out of 3) in the United States are circumcised. It is not clear whether this confers any long-term health benefit. What is clear is that complications emerge in about 1 in every 5,000 circumcisions; 2 deaths occur for every 1 million operations performed.

A black woman in the United States is 4 times more likely to die in childbirth than a white woman.

9

A Potpourri
of Risks

This last chapter, inevitably, is a grabbag or catchall of interesting risks that do not fall neatly into the categories examined in earlier chapters. Although ranging far afield, the principal risks under review here include those associated with transportation, nature and the environment, crime, education, and smoking.

GETTING THERE BY CAR

Likelihood that a motor vehicle accident is principally caused by driver error (as opposed to vehicle defects): 98.5%. For purposes of comparison, the likelihood that a plane crash is caused by pilot error is about 67%.

When vehicle defects do play a role in automobile accidents, faulty brakes and tires are the leading culprits.

In a significant number of service stations, both the regular *and* the premium gas pumps are connected to the *same* underground tank.

Every year about 25,000 emergency vehicles (police cars, fire trucks, and ambulances) are involved in accidents, 1% of which are fatal.

Proportion of drivers on the road *after dark* who are legally intoxicated: 1 in 25.

In those states that have introduced stiff laws requiring mandatory jail time for those convicted of driving under the influence in a first offense, the number of driving fatalities due to drunk driving has decreased an astonishing 2%!

One generally finds the largest number of drunk drivers on the roads during holiday periods. Not surprisingly, New Year's Eve sees the highest proportion, followed (in order) by Thanksgiving and Memorial Day.

In 1989, Britain introduced a law requiring children riding in the backseat of a car to wear a seat belt. The following year, the number of deaths and injuries to children in vehicle backseats *increased* by 10%.

The National Highway Traffic Safety Commission has recent-ly issued a warning that air bags can kill or seriously injure children who are not wearing seat belts as well as babies in infant seats. For instance, air bags cause about 800 serious, potentially fatal, injuries to infants every year. As airbags become more common, these numbers will rise. (Despite this, all new cars must be fitted by air bags no later than 1997.)

For every fatal automobile accident, there are 12 involving serious injury. For every serious accident, there are 6 involv-ing slight injury. In other words, there are 70 accidents involving slight injury for every fatal accident.

Safety backfires again! About 5 million motor vehicles are recalled in the United States each year for safety-related defects. If the average American lives about 5 miles from the dealership, we can confidently predict that, directly as a result of the safety recall, there will be at least 1 fatal crash and 50 or so disabling injuries, all resulting from the fact that 5 million drivers are making a single round-trip to their local garage ostensibly in the name of safety.

Car with the highest *rate* of theft in the United States: Mercedes SL convertible. Car most frequently stolen: Honda Accord.

One way of lowering the risk of your new car being stolen is to buy a newly designed model. Because its parts are less interchangeable with previous models, thieves are about 10% less likely to steal it than they are a new vehicle that is a carryover from previous years.

The next time she suggests selling the Jag and buying diamonds, remind her: Chances that a stolen car will be recovered: 65%. That stolen jewelry will be found: 5%.

Experiments indicate that the safest car colors are blue in daylight and yellow at night. If you drive in both conditions, white is overall the most visible. The riskiest car colors are gray and dark green.

Probability of having a serious injury if you crash your car at 35 miles per hour: 20%. Ten years ago: closer to 50%.

A driver who is a diabetic with severe hypoglycemia reactions is 19 times more likely to have a crash than an average driver.

RISK ENHANCERS

Your risk of being in a traffic fatality is heightened if you:

- are 16–24
- are over 75
- are divorced
- are a police officer
- are a man
- have drunk *any* alcohol
- drive a small car
- don't wear seat belts
- exceed speed limits
- drive at night

Before that inclines you to think that we shouldn't issue driver's licenses to such folks, bear in mind that their accident
rate, bad as it is, is still better than that of a healthy, 18-year-
old, male driver.

RISK GEOGRAPHY

Percentage of road bridges
in New York State rated as
deficient: 71%.

Studies suggest that a good
cure for motion sickness is to
shut your eyes frequently. The
idea is that a part of the sense
of nausea develops from your
eyes telling you that you're
moving when your body says the opposite, or vice versa.
This remedy is not a good idea if you are the driver!

On highways still posted as having a speed limit of 55 miles
per hour, the average vehicle is traveling 60–65; 1 in 10
vehicles is speeding more than 10 miles per hour above the
posted limit.

On a highway, the likelihood of a crash increases the further
your speed departs—in *either* direction—from that of other
drivers. This means that going, say, 10 miles per hour slower
than average puts you as much at risk for a collision as going
10 miles per hour faster does.

Many drivers tend to suppose that modern highways are all
of a piece from a safety point of view. Far from it; the safest
highways (usually urban ones) are almost 1,000% safer than
the most dangerous ones (usually rural).

During the period 1990–94, the Volvo 240 had the lowest
death rate: about 1 fatality per 100,000 vehicles. At the
other extreme, the Chevrolet Corvette had 30 deaths per
100,000 vehicles. (Strangely, though, the Corvette had a
lower-than-average injury rate.)

Riding in a car with a male driver is 250% more likely to kill you than if the driver is female.

Almost always, spending dollars to avoid one kind of risk means fewer dollars available to avoid others. The trade-offs we make are not always sensible. For instance, numerous studies show that, dollar for-dollar, money spent on improving highway design saves more lives than money spent on emergency medical vehicles. Notwithstanding, most Americans say they would much rather see our money invested in more ambulances than in better roads.

Recent studies show that in highway driving the per-mile accident rate is much higher for curves than for straightaways. That will surprise few of us. What you may not realize is that left-curving highways are 60% more dangerous than right-curving ones.

The highway accident rate per mile is twice as great on hills as it is on flat highway.

Ever wonder why teenage drivers get hit with such high auto insurance premiums? Ponder the fact that a 16-year-old male driver is about 40 times more dangerous on the highways than a 40-year-old woman. The truth is that the high added premiums usually charged to teenage drivers, especially males, do not begin to reflect how dangerous they are. Everyone else is paying extra premiums to subsidize this group's notoriously bad driving record.

RISK GEOGRAPHY

State where car drivers are most likely to be legally drunk: New Mexico. Most likely to be sober: Delaware.

Women are generally safer drivers than men until about the age of 35. Thereafter, men win the driving safety sweepstakes. The safest driver on the road is a 42-year-old man.

Lest older readers are beginning to feel smug on this score, they should bear in mind that both men and women over the age of about 65 have an accident record that rivals those in their late teens—the only difference being that, among the seniors, women exhibit the worse driving record, whereas younger men win the booby prize.

Vehicle weight is another crucial determinant of crash survivability. In fact, if the driver of a very heavy car has a head-on collision with a very light car, the heavyweight driver is 20 times more likely to survive the crash than the other driver.

Insurance industry claims figures reveal a similar pattern. Heavy utility vehicles, estate wagons, large luxury cars, and vans generally have lower injury loss figures than other vehicle types. Small four-door cars have one of the worst injury ratings.

Another side of the weight advantage shows up if we compare fatalities in accidents involving commercial trucks and passenger vehicles. If a truck is involved in a fatal crash, the likelihood that the truck driver is the fatality (as opposed to the hapless car driver) is only about 20%.

In fact, you are less likely to be a highway fatality if you drive a large car *without* a seat belt than if you drive a small one *with* a seat belt.

What these comparisons boil down to is this: Smaller cars kill about 3,500 people each year who would not have died had they been in a larger vehicle.

Chances that a public road in the United States is unpaved: 1%. In Canada: 75%.

Chance that your car's head restraint will *not* be effective at protecting your neck in a rear-end collision: 96%.

Odds that you will get whiplash this year: 1 in 2,000.

Likelihood that a car you are driving will someday hit a pedestrian: 4%.

Proportion of pedestrians injured in a collision who are drunk: 1 in 2.

RISK GEOGRAPHY

Riskiest state in which to be a pedestrian: New Mexico.

Sometimes blow your fuse over "Sunday drivers"? They may be slow, but they're relatively safe. The fact is that, per passenger mile driven, your risk of a fatal crash on every other day of the week is generally about 8 times higher than it is on Sunday.

The average medical bill for a highway injury is about $6,000.

Prior to 1986, daylight saving time started the last Sunday of April. In that year, it was moved up to the first Sunday in April. This shift of a few weeks saves about 20 lives per year, mostly schoolchildren and other pedestrians.

GETTING THERE OTHERWISE

If you fly 100,000 miles per year in large, commercial jets, your annual odds of dying in a plane crash is about 1 in 500,000.

On *commuter* airlines, the risk is about 10 times as great, that is, about 1 in 50,000.

RISK GEOGRAPHY

Odds that a flight leaving Newark, JFK, or Chicago will be delayed: 3 to 1.

If you fly that far in *private* planes or large helicopters, your odds are about 1 in 5,000.

Chances that you will be bumped from your next flight: 1 in 4,000.

The U.S. airlines with the best safety records in the last 15 years:

- TWA
- Southwest
- Alaska
- America West
- Hawaiian

In 1992, the five largest U.S. airlines reported 150 incidents in which a pilot seriously violated federal aviation regulations.

RISK GEOGRAPHY

According to pilots' associations, the most dangerous commercial airports in the United States are San Francisco and Los Angeles.

This comes from the "No Risk Is Too Remote to Calculate Department": Your odds of dying from a plane falling on you this year: 1 in 25 million.

Virtually all forms of public transportation are safer than the private motor car. Specifically, per passenger mile, planes, trains, and buses have a fatality rate that is only about 2% that of the passenger car. (Commuter flights have risk profiles similar to those of a safe driver.)

A rider or passenger on a motorbike is 16 times more likely to meet a nasty end than someone riding in an automobile a comparable distance.

Odds that you will be injured this year if you ride a motorcycle: 1 in 68.

RISK GEOGRAPHY
Riskiest state in which to ride a motorcycle: Wyoming.

Odds that a motorcyclist will have a fatal accident this year: 1 in 1,600.

According to the National Highway Traffic Safety Administration, helmet use saves the lives of about 500–600 injured motorcyclists each year, reducing the risk of a fatal accident by about one-third.

Three-quarters of bicyclists never wear a helmet, even though more than 10% of cycle-related injuries involve damage to the head.

RISK GEOGRAPHY
Riskiest state in which to ride a bicycle: Florida.

If you ride a bicycle this year, the odds of

- serious injury: 1 in 1,000
- a fatal accident: 1 in 80,000

For every *hour* you spend bicycling, your chance of serious injury is about 1 in 25,000.

MOTHER NATURE

Odds that you will be driven from your home this year by a flood: 1 in 4,000.

The average tornado moves with a forward speed of about 40 miles per hour. Its winds average about 110 miles per hour. It typically arrives from the southwest. Its touch-down path is about 2 miles long, and its width is about 1,200 feet.

Despite repeated claims to the contrary, controlled studies have not been able to find a link between a full moon and unusual behavior.

An El Niño is a humongous pool of warm water that moves for several months from the western Pacific toward the Americas. They develop about 1 year in 3. Hurricanes and tropical storms are twice as likely to develop in the Pacific during El Niño years than otherwise. Interestingly, the Atlantic tends to have fewer such storms than normal during El Niño years in the Pacific.

Space debris: NASA estimates that currently in earth orbit are more than 10,000 objects larger than a softball, any one of which could produce catastrophic consequences if it collided with a manned spacecraft.

If you free-fall through a long descent, your speed of fall gradually increases until it reaches a terminal velocity of about 120 miles per hour. If you fall headfirst, the terminal velocity is closer to 175 miles per hour.

> ### RISK GEOGRAPHY
>
> State with the lowest record high temperature: Hawaii (100 degrees Fahrenheit).
>
> State with the highest record low temperature: Hawaii (14 degrees Fahrenheit).

Everyone knows that being immersed in frigid arctic waters rapidly produces unconsciousness and, soon thereafter, death. Less well known is the fact that much warmer water will produce comparable effects over longer periods. For instance, you may become unconscious after being immersed in water for:

- 30 minutes at 40 degrees Fahrenheit
- 1 hour at 50 degrees Fahrenheit
- 2 hours at 60 degrees Fahrenheit.

RISK GEOGRAPHY

Rainiest major city in the United States: Miami, Florida.

Cloudiest city in the United States: a dead heat between Cleveland, Ohio, and Columbus, Ohio.

Sunniest large U.S. city: Phoenix, Arizona.

Roughly one-third of deaths due to drowning involve persons whose autopsies reveal no excess water in the lungs. The actual cause of death in such cases is suffocation. Here, in a kind of reflex action, the muscles of the windpipe seal it shut before water enters.

Acts of God: Freak turns in the weather claim the lives of hundreds of Americans every year. Here, in order of *decreasing* severity, are some of the principal killers:

- snow or ice
- floods
- lightning
- tornadoes
- hurricanes
- heat waves

Other natural killers—which are not weather-related— include volcanic eruptions, earthquakes, tsunamis (tidal waves), avalanches, land subsidence, meteors, freak releases of subterranean or subaqueous gases, and solar and terrestrial radiation (especially radon gas).

THE BIG ONE

When a landslide occurs above a lake or bay, it can produce a wave of gigantic proportions. One such landslide into Lituya Bay, Alaska, in 1958 produced a wave more than 1,500 feet high.

Those most likely to die in a major earthquake:

- children ages 5–9
- seniors 60+

> ### RISK FACTORS
>
> An animal species is less likely to survive if its members:
>
> - are large in size
> - have a valuable fur, oil, and so forth
> - have a narrow habitat tolerance
> - have long gestation periods
> - produce small litters
> - are dangerous to humans

In a strong earthquake (6.5–7.4 on the Richter scale), there will be about 3 serious injuries for every fatality.

Odds of a thunderstorm in the southeastern United States on any given day: 1 in 4.

Chance that you are sensitive to poison ivy: 85%.

You are 9 times more likely to be seriously bitten by a dog than by a cat.

The so-called fire ant found its way into the United States from South America in the late 1930s. Since that time, more than 40 deaths have been attributed to fire ant stings, mostly in Florida and Texas. Although deaths are rare, about 2% of those stung develop acute and severe allergic reactions.

Other feared insects generally have more benign records. The tarantula spider, for instance, is nontoxic. It can sting but its sting is not venomous. Scorpions and black widows produce nasty stings that *can* be fatal, but they almost never are. Far more Americans die from bee stings than from the predations of all spiders and scorpions.

The phobia you are most likely to have: fear of spiders (arachnophobia).

Among redback spiders (common in Australia), the female is 50 times larger than the male. Two-thirds of the time, she eats the male during copulation.

The preferred lair of the crab louse is human pubic hair. Roughly 1–2% of us has such an infestation at any given time.

Many people have tiny itch mites (scabies) on their body. The average person infected has about 10 mites. Most common sites of infestation: hands, elbows, feet, scrotum, and penis.

Some people still think of scabies as a type of venereal disease. It is nothing of the sort, although—given one of its common sites of infestation—it can move from one host to another during sexual contact.

The pain of a flying insect sting, in *increasing* severity, is:

- honeybee
- bumblebee
- wasp
- hornet

Pound-for-pound, spider venom is much more potent than rattlesnake venom. Fortunately, spiders carry much less of it around than snakes do.

Odds that you'll be bitten this year by a poisonous snake: 1 in 40,000.

A shark can detect the presence of blood in seawater in quantities as small as 1 part per million.

Of those life forms known to have existed (which are only a small proportion of those that probably have existed), those that are still extant: 0.01%.

Cost of raising the average dog for 10 years: $5,000+.

Percentage of dogs that are overweight: 40%.

OF LICE AND MEN

Insects are the principal carriers of many dreaded diseases. Among them are:

mosquitoes	yellow fever, malaria, equine encephalitis
ticks	Rocky Mountain spotted fever
lice, mites	typhus
fleas	plague
roaches	salmonella

ENVIRONMENT TRADE-OFFS

Found your allergies increasing lately? Apt to blame your local polluting industry? Before you do, you might ponder the fact that energy-saving measures recommended or mandated by the Environmental Protection Agency and the Occupational Safety and Health Administration over the years have reduced the number of air changes in a house or small office building from about 4 changes per hour to about 1 per day. Dust mites—to which many of us are allergic—flourish in such circumstances.

A pollution paradox: All of us have read about how the depletion in the ozone layer threatens to dramatically increase the frequency of skin cancers, including fatal ones. What is less well known is that, along with the ozone layer, one of the major filters of cancer-causing ultraviolet radiation is air pollution. Accordingly, as we clean up the air in our cities, we inadvertently increase UV exposure levels, just as surely as (and probably more dramatically than) ozone holes in the upper atmosphere do.

Average number of nuclear power plants in your state: 2.

Annual cost to the average U.S. family of compliance with federal safety and environmental regulations: $4,000.

RISK GEOGRAPHY

During the 1980s, New Jersey generated 40% of all the hazardous waste in the United States. Not surprisingly, New Jersey has more EPA Superfund sites (90) than any other state.

The average cost of collecting and then sorting 1 pound of recyclable waste is $0.09. The value of the recycled material, once sorted, is about $0.02.

One average annual subscription to a daily newspaper produces about 550 pounds of wastepaper.

Oil spills in cold regions of the globe are almost always more serious than elsewhere because the natural processes of biodegradation are dramatically slower in colder waters.

When zoologists study bird populations relative to centers of human habitation, they generally find that, although *fewer* species thrive in urban areas than in rural ones, the number and density of birds is about 7 times greater in the former than in the latter. In other words, a human presence tends to increase the bird population but to decrease the biological diversity.

In the interest of protecting endangered species, the federal government spends $5 million on every living Florida panther.

Experts generally agree that somewhere between 2 and 3% of all cancers are associated with environmental pollution. This obviously means that even if we could *completely* elimi-

nate pollution (which is probably unrealistic), we would be preventing only a tiny fraction of the 500,000 annual deaths due to cancer.

Some men working in the plastics industry develop large breasts. Scientists speculate that a chemical released from plastic at high temperature behaves as an estrogen and is inhaled in large quantities by some plastics workers.

A Florida study indicates that male alligators, exposed to large quantities of DDT, develop unusually small penises.

Urban climates differ significantly from surrounding rural ones. During the winter, for instance, a typical city will be about 3–5 degrees Fahrenheit warmer than the surrounding countryside. Wind speeds in cities are about two-thirds that of the outlying regions. Cities will be about 10% cloudier and 5–10% rainier than the countryside.

These changes—slightly warmer and slightly wetter—correspond approximately to what experts predict that a century's worth of greenhouse effect warming would do to most regions of the globe. So, if you want a preview of the climate a century from now in your region, spend a few days in one of its larger cities.

According to the EPA, U.S. industry releases about 250–300 million tons of toxic chemicals each year. They break down as follows:

- 100,000 tons into the water
- 120 million tons into the air

- 250,000 tons into landfills
- 60 million tons into underground wells
- 250,000 tons into wastewater treatment plants
- 50 million tons into waste disposal facilities

Just as artificial sources of radiation (for example, X rays or nuclear power plants) can add small increments to the possibility that you will die from cancer, *naturally occurring radiation* can have the same effect. This comes from a variety of sources, principally the sun and radioactive decay of natural substances like radon. Much of our protection against the sun's rays (cosmic radiation) comes from the thickness of the atmosphere, which filters out most of the dangerous rays. However, as we go to altitudes well above sea level, the atmosphere obviously affords less protection. For instance, a 10-hour trip in a jet at 35,000 feet increases your chances of a fatal cancer by about 1 in 1 million over what the odds would be if you spent your time at sea level.

A stay of 2 months or so in Denver will have about the same effect. (Before you make any resolutions about avoiding places like Denver, bear in mind that Colorado has a much lower cancer death rate than the U.S. average—which goes to show that radiation is one, but not the principal, cause of cancer.)

In the same vein, you NIMBYs (not in my backyard) out there should know that most of the states with active uranium mines and mills (such as New Mexico, Colorado, and Wyoming) have lower cancer rates than the national average.

In a Harvard survey of 1,000 scientists, fewer than half (42%) thought that the EPA's method of establishing environmental standards is scientifically sound.

CRIME AND GUNS

Your risk of being the victim of a shooting accident is heightened if you are:

- Protestant
- male
- white

Proportion of those who have died, ages 1–34, whose death was caused by firearms: 18%.

Your risk of becoming a murderer is heightened if you are:

- divorced, single, or separated
- male
- black
- poor

Number of assault weapons in private hands in the United States: almost 1 million.

Odds that a student often carries a weapon—a gun or knife—to school: 22%.

During a career in the classroom, 1 in 10 public school teachers will be physically assaulted by a student.

You are more likely to be a rape victim if you are:

RISK GEOGRAPHY

State where a woman is most likely to be raped: Alaska. Least likely: North Dakota.

- female
- under 25
- poor
- black
- away from home

Percentage of parents with guns in the home who do not keep them under lock and key: 50%.

Odds that you will be shot to death this year by a police officer in the line of duty: 1 in 1 million.

You are more likely to become a murder victim if you are:

- male
- black
- divorced or separated
- aged 15–25

RISK GEOGRAPHY

State where you're most likely to be murdered: Washington, D.C. Least likely: North Dakota.

Odds that someone 15–24 will be killed by a firearm this year: 1 in 350. (Roughly 40% of these deaths are suicides.) For black men of this age group, the risk of death by firearms is closer to 1 in 80.

The fairy tales were right after all: Children under 2 are 50 times more likely to be killed by a stepparent than by a natural parent.

Odds that a prisoner will escape from jail this year: 1 in 75.

Odds that a federal prison inmate will escape this year: 1 in 200.

RISK GEOGRAPHY

Someone living in California is 20 times more likely to be a drug dealer than a resident of South Carolina is.

One in every 4 prison deaths is due to AIDS.

Odds that a prisoner on death row will have his or her sentence overturned or commuted: 2 in 5.

Average cost (including appeals) for each convicted murderer executed: $3 million.

With that sum, one could incarcerate the felon in a maximum security prison for more than 35 years.

RISK GEOGRAPHY

Folks are most likely to carry a concealed weapon in Missouri and Wisconsin. Guns are least likely in Vermont.

Ever wonder how arsenic gained its reputation as the poison of choice? The answer is simple: If administered in small doses over a period of time, arsenic poisoning exhibits symptoms that are easily confused with ordinary, if serious, diseases: loss of appetite, nausea, vomiting, hair loss, bronchitis, and vascular disorders. Until the emergence of modern analytic chemistry, it was virtually impossible to distinguish arsenic poisoning from many commonplace disorders.

Percentage of emergency room visits where the injury is violence related: 6%.

RISK GEOGRAPHY

Someone living in Louisiana is 7 times more likely to wind up in prison as someone in North Dakota.

Among blacks and whites convicted of similar crimes, blacks generally receive sentences that are 10% longer.

Each year about 20,000 children give evidence in child abuse trials. Research indicates that when children are repeatedly questioned about an event that never happened, about half of them develop false memories about the event, eventually coming to believe its truth.

RISK GEOGRAPHY

City with the highest crime rate: Atlanta

Most of us, in the wake of the bombing of the Federal Building in Oklahoma City, tend to suppose that domestic terrorism in the United States is a phenomenon of the 1990s. Things, we assure ourselves, didn't used to be this way. Well, the data suggest otherwise. During the 1980s, for instance, the United States

had a score of political assas-
sinations, more than 100
politically motivated bomb-
ings, almost 50 hijackings of
aircraft, and a handful of
episodes of sabotage and
hostage-taking by those with
a political ax to grind.

RISK GEOGRAPHY

Judging by arrest dockets, a
person from Kentucky is 9
times more likely to be a sex
offender than someone from
South Carolina is.

Double Jeopardy? Odds that a condemned prisoner will
have his or her execution botched on the first try: 8%.

A LITTLE LEARNING IS A DANGEROUS THING

The high-school dropout rate of white and black youths is
virtually identical at 5%.

Nonetheless, studies by the National Assessment of
Educational Progress, which tracks educational patterns in
the United States, claim that only about 20% of black
17-year-olds were able to read at an "adept" level. About half
the white youths of that age can read adeptly.

Odds that a student receiving a high-school diploma will
lack minimal reading skills: 1 in 7.

Chances that a child will dislike school: 1 in 3.

Percentage of U.S. sixth-graders who cannot locate the
United States on a world map: 80%.

Percentage of U.S. adults who cannot understand the
instructions on a bottle of aspirin: 20%.

Chance that he or she cannot work out what a weather chart
in the newspaper means: 25%.

According to the U.S. Department of Education, barely half the adult population can make sense of a bus or train schedule.

Odds that a U.S. high school *graduate* will be unable to pass a seventh-grade arithmetic exam: 50–50.

Percentage of children living with a single parent who will have to repeat a grade in school: 30%.

Percentage of children living with both parents who will fail a grade: 10%.

Someone with a bachelor's degree is likely to earn about 65% more than a high-school graduate of the same age. Having an advanced degree produces an annual income more than twice as high as that of the high-school graduate.

Average yearly tuition (exclusive of room and board) at a first-rate U.S. private college or university: $15,000.

In recent years, the chances of being accepted by some select colleges if you apply have been these:

Harvard College	15%
Princeton and Stanford	16%
Yale	18%
Massachusetts Institute of Technology	24%
Cornell	29%
California Institute of Technology	31%
Chicago	47%

Chances that a random undergraduate will eventually receive a Ph.D. degree: 1 in 30 (1 in 10 Princeton undergraduates will earn a doctorate.)

Chance that a child in grade school will regularly be left alone at home: 4%.

Education and health: someone who drops out of high school is 3 times more likely to die between the ages of 25 and 44 than a college graduate. Between 45 and 64, the dropout is twice as likely to die as the college graduate.

LIGHTING UP

Both nonsmokers and smokers believe that smoking is likely to kill you. The fact is that *most* smokers die, when they die, of diseases unrelated to their smoking.

The biggest single threat from smoking is lung cancer. Smokers are hundreds of times more likely to get it than nonsmokers. Still, the fact is that a smoker—even a heavy smoker—is much more likely *not* to get lung cancer than to get it.

Specifically, a cigarette smoker's annual risk of lung cancer is about 1 in 250.

There are plenty of other nasty risks associated with cigarette smoking, as the accompanying box makes clear. But the popular impression—promoted by the media and the U.S. Surgeon General alike—that smokers are knowingly committing some type of suicide every time they light up is a hyperbolic exaggeration of the known health effects of smoking.

According to official figures from the Environmental Protection Agency, the annual likelihood that a nonsmoker living and working around smokers will die of lung cancer from exposure to their smoke is about 1 in 80,000. A year's exposure to secondhand smoke poses about the same level of risk of death as you run driving your car around town for a couple of weeks.

If a female smoker stops smoking, she adds about 8 months to her life expectancy. A man who quits adds about 10 months.

> ## A SHORT LIST OF SMOKING'S DANGERS
>
> Among the many ill effects of cigarette smoking, these are perhaps the most serious. Smoking increases the risk of:
>
> - lung, mouth, bladder, and throat cancers
> - heart disease
> - stroke
> - pregnancy complications
> - emphysema
>
> Smoking roughly doubles your risk of premature death.

About one-third of black adults over the age of 26 smoke cigarettes, compared to roughly one-fourth of white adults. We get a very different picture, however, when we look at teenage smokers; while 1 in 5 white teens smokes regularly, only 1 in 25 black teens does.

Public discussions on smoking these days tend to focus exclusively on the cigarette smoker. The fact is that 5% of the male population smokes cigars and pipes while another 6% chews tobacco or uses snuff. These groups run only 10% of the risk of premature death of the cigarette smoker.

Odds that you use pot: 1 in 10.

Odds that you are addicted to heroin: 1 in 500.

TOO MISCELLANEOUS TO CLASSIFY

Chances that, if you take the qualifying exam to appear on *Jeopardy*, you will eventually appear on the show: 1 in 44.

Chance that some of the software on your personal computer is bootlegged: 50%.

Chance that when you next switch on your television, a commercial will be airing: 22%.

Since the collapse of communism in the Soviet Union, the life expectancy for Russian men has fallen 6 years, to 58.5, and 5.5 years for Russian women, to 68.5.

A white man over the age of 75 is 10 times more likely to commit suicide than a white woman of the same age.

Amount of time you will spend in line today: 20 minutes.

Odds that when you die you will be cremated: 1 in 5.

Speaking of what happens to you after you die: Only 1 in 12 Americans expects to go to hell.

Items you are most likely to lose on the New York subway (in descending order):

- backpack
- radio
- glasses

Odds that an illegal alien trying to cross the border will be caught: 1 in 4.

Odds that someone trying to smuggle marijuana or cocaine into the United States will be apprehended: 1 in 10.

Many Americans suppose that the United States lost far more MIAs during the Vietnam War than in other campaigns. The fact is that an American serviceman during World War II was 1,600% more likely to be declared Missing in Action than his counterpart in Vietnam.

Approximate amount that the United States spent *each year* from 1985–1995 in its efforts to resolve the remaining cases of MIAs in Vietnam: $100,000,000. Number of unresolved cases: 55.

Number of Americans who share your birthday (unless you were born on February 29th): more than 700,000.

Some 10,000 Americans were born on the same day as you in the same year. Odds that the next person you meet will come in the latter category: about 1 in 25,000.

Risk that your aged mother will someday come to live with you: 11%. Your father: 6%.

Odds that you will live within an hour's travel time of your aging parents: 75%.

Odds that, in your old age, you will have no close friends: 1 in 5.

Odds that you will one day receive a new identity under the U.S. Witness Security Program: 1 in 20,000.

Chances that a large rocket, of the sort used to put satellites into orbit, will fail: 5%.

Odds that a random dream will be a nightmare: 1 in 1,500.

Chances that you will go to Walt Disney World this year: 1 in 10. To Las Vegas: 1 in 12.

Odds that nuclear weapons are based in your home state: 50%.

Odds of being injured or killed in a single trip on an elevator: 1 in 17 million.

Sources

A book like this can be no better than the numbers in it. For those numbers, I am indebted to literally thousands of anonymous epidemiologists, statisticians, actuaries, criminologists, designers of clinical trials, and the rest of the risk industry who work laboriously accumulating data. So far as possible, I have drawn on studies that are both timely and robust, but the various means by which experts make estimates of risk vary enormously from subject to subject. Even within the same subject, and even when risk investigators agree on the appropriate methods, different trials sometimes give quite divergent results. Moreover, the character of the risks themselves changes, as we find new ways of curing disease, cleaning the environment, or fighting crime. Some of the risk numbers quoted here emerged from elaborately designed trials or extensive epidemiological analysis and are probably highly reliable. Others simply represent rough-and-ready extrapolations from observed relative frequencies and are thus more impressionistic than scientific. Moreover, almost all describe the levels of risk for that purely hypothetical creature, the average American. For such reasons, the figures here should be handled with a skepticism appropriate to the recognition that our understanding of many risks is still in a pretty primitive state.

It would be impossible to acknowledge individually all of the sources on which I have drawn in putting this volume together. What follows is a stab at identifying the more important and frequently utilized among them.

CHAPTER I

As there are almost no risk data contained in this introductory chapter, there is no need for a long list of sources and credits. What should be said is that many of these rules of thumb for thinking about risk were first hammered out in articles and columns I wrote for the magazine *Consumers' Research*, must reading for anyone concerned with the risks of ordinary life.

CHAPTER 2

Most of the information about economic risks comes from the U.S. Census Bureau, the Department of Labor, and the Bureau of Labor Statistics. Other sources include:

Centers for Disease Control

CQ Researcher

Dun & Bradstreet

The Economist

Federal Deposit Insurance Corporation

The Investment Institute

National Agricultural Statistics Service

National Safety Council

Scarne, J., *Scarne's New Complete Guide to Gambling* (New York: Simon & Shuster, 1974)

Statistical Handbook on the American Family (Phoenix, Ariz.: Oryx Press, 1993)

U.S. Department of Commerce

CHAPTER 3

The bulk of the information on risks associated with sex came from the National Center for Health Statistics and the Centers for Disease Control. Also useful have been:

American Journal of Public Health

Blumstein, R. and P. Schwartz, *American Couples* (New York: Morrow, 1983)

Brookmeyer, Ron, *AIDS Epidemiology* (Oxford, England: Oxford University Press, 1994)

Collins, R., *Sociology of Marriage and the Family* (Chicago: Nelson-Hall, 1991)

Consumers Union

Diamond, S., and M. Maliszewski, ed., *Sexual Aspects of Headaches* (Madison, Conn.: International Universities Press, 1992)

Institute of Sexual Research, Indiana University

National Institute of Child Health and Human Development

Nature

Science

Statistical Handbook on the American Family (Phoenix, Ariz.: Oryx Press, 1993)

University of Michigan School of Public Health

U.S. Department of Justice

CHAPTER 4

Much of our information about food risk comes, of course, from the U.S. Department of Agriculture and the Food and Drug Administration. To my mind, the best popular source of general information about food risk is *Consumers' Research*. Data have also been drawn from:

American Journal of Clinical Nutrition

American Journal of Epidemiology

Brostoff, J., *Food Allergy* (London: Brailliere, 1987)

Centers for Disease Control

Consumers Union

The Distilled Spirits Council

Geissler, C., *Food, Diet and Economic Change* (Leicester: Leicester University Press, 1993)

International Bottled Water Association

Journal of the American Medical Association

Lessot, M., *Food Intolerance* (London: Chapman & Hall, 1992)

National Center for Health Statistics

National Institute on Drug Abuse

National Safety Council

U.S. Department of Health and Human Services

CHAPTER 5

The U.S. government has some splendid agencies promulgating data about health risks. Most important are the National Institutes of Health, the Centers for Disease Control, and the National Center for Health Statistics. Most of the risk data in this chapter are derived from these three sources. Other helpful sources include:

Alfin-Slater, R., *Cancer and Nutrition* (New York: Plenum, 1991).

American Association of Plastic Surgeons

American Cancer Society

American Hospital Association

Archives of General Psychiatry

Consumer Reports

The Economist

Journal of the American Medical Association

Journal of Occupational Medicine

Lancet

National Academy of Engineering

Science

U.S. Department of Health and Human Services

CHAPTER 6

No one knows as much about risks around the house as the people at the Consumer Products Safety Commission, who regularly issue detailed reports about home accidents and risks. I have drawn very heavily in this chapter on their data. In addition, information here comes from:

Appliance Magazine

Consumers Union

The Economist

Journal of Occupational Medicine

Nater, J., ed., *Unwanted Effects of Cosmetics* (Amsterdam: Excerpta Medica, 1983)

National Center for Health Statistics

Risk Analysis

U.S. Public Health Service

The Wellness Letter

CHAPTER 7

Here again, the Consumer Product Safety Commission tracks many sports injuries. Other data on the safety of various leisure activities come from various athletic associations and from the National Safety Council.

CHAPTER 8

Most of the data here came from the U.S. Census Bureau and the National Center for Health Statistics. I also made extensive use of P. Blumenstein, *American Couples* (New York: Morrow, 1983).

CHAPTER 9
....

Being a miscellaneous chapter, the data here came from very disparate sources. Among the more important are these:

Bureau of Labor Statistics

Center for Study of Social Policy

Centers for Disease Control

Consumer Product Safety Commission

Consumers' Research

CQ Researcher

The Distilled Spirits Council

The Gerontologist

Goude, A., *The Human Impact* (Cambridge: MIT Press, 1994)

Institute for Social Research, University of Michigan

National Highway Traffic Safety Administration

National Institute for Occupational Safety and Health

National Safety Council

National Transportation Safety Board

National Oceanic and Atmospheric Administration

National Weather Service

New York Transit Authority

Risk Analysis

Science

Statistical Abstracts of the United States

U-Haul Rental

U.S. Census Bureau

U.S. Drug Enforcement Agency

U.S. Justice Department

U.S. Transportation Department

Whipple, C., *De Minimis Risk* (New York: Plenum, 1987)

Index